What We Learn
from Children

WHAT WE LEARN FROM CHILDREN

Professor of Educational Psychology
Wayne University

MARIE I. RASEY, PH.D.

AND

J. W. MENGE, PH.D.

Professor of Education
Wayne University

HARPER & BROTHERS: NEW YORK

WHAT WE LEARN FROM CHILDREN
Copyright, 1956, by Harper & Brothers ©
Printed in the United States of America

All rights in this book are reserved.
No part of the book may be used or reproduced
in any manner whatsoever without written permission except in the case of brief quotations
embodied in critical articles and reviews. For
information address Harper & Brothers
49 East 33rd Street, New York 16, N. Y.

FIRST EDITION
M-E

Library of Congress catalog card number: 55-8544

To our students who have been our teachers

CONTENTS

CONTENTS

FOREWORD

by C. J. Marinus, M.D.

For the last ten years I have had the unique privilege of watching the impact of a dedicated mind upon the problems involved in the nurture of mentally handicapped and emotionally disturbed children.

Marie Rasey is that mind, peculiarly gifted for the task at hand. I should like to point out a few facets of her personality that have made possible the contribution that she has made and is making.

Marie is a humble person, who knows that she does not know all the answers. For this reason she is able to observe a fact, interpret it fairly, even though this means changing her previous hypotheses and procedures.

She is motivated by an unshaken love of people, particularly of the little people, whether little in the eyes of the world, or little in point of stature.

One of her important assets is a complete absence of emotional reaction to the faults of her children. She is not disturbed by the temper tantrums, the destructiveness, the antisocial acts of the emotionally disturbed or retarded child. The broken window or the soiled clothing do not fill her with anger or disgust, but she is interested in *why* the act occurred. Patient delving into the mind of the "bad boy" to find out why he wanted to commit the "crime" progresses uninhibited by her own emotions. As you will see from the case histories, the correct answer was often discovered.

With her fine background of theoretic and practical psychology, alive and warm and human, she has been able to translate an astonishing number of incidents into the elements of a pattern.

Thirty years ago medical diagnosis was directed toward the

finding of pathology, a single disease that would account for all the symptoms observed in the sick patient. Today medical diagnosis strives to find, in addition, the factor of pathological physiology which became an integral part in the sickness of the patient. Treatment of the abnormal physiological reactions is added to the direct attack upon the underlying pathology—the diseased state.

Dr. Rasey's program follows this same technique. In every child under her care the emotional sickness, the nutrition, the endocrine status, the physical condition, the social maladjustments must be studied, and the program is not complete unless all factors which *might* alter the child's total effectiveness as an organism are analyzed and "treated" insofar as possible.

And finally Dr. Rasey has a God-given gift of putting on paper observation, facts, ideas, in such a way that the reader sees and feels and lives the story as she does.

PREFACE

Twenty years can be a long time. It was twenty years ago that Rayswift came into being. Dr. Edith Hale Swift and Marie I. Rasey, working jointly in Detroit on parental and child problems, came to that place, well known to many, when the pursuit of objections and anxieties and expectations for a better world can no longer implement themselves with words and teaching with words. Something, we felt, must be done about it. Our naïve outlook in the early thirties seems childish now. It was that if somehow teachers, social workers, doctors, and workers with youth could be brought into the comparative peace of a country environment, and be set down to think together, many problems which bedeviled workers with children could be brought to solution.

Neither of us realized that the problems which troubled us were not local in origin, nor would local efforts solve them. There was to follow evidence aplenty that it was the world which was sick, and not alone Detroit. Nonetheless we began to make our ideas take on reality of place and purpose and rapidly move into the realm of the actual.

The old house took on new sturdiness. Kitchens and living room space were doubled. The accumulated weeds and refuse of years gave way to tidiness. Tulips and daffodil bulbs went in and on December 29 of 1934 a group of friends came to help us dedicate ourselves and it.

The fireplace carried an inscription on its thick oak mantel, EVERY LOVELINESS, for we were both confident that loveliness could crowd out hatefulness, beauty could master ugliness, and courage cast out fear. We also knew that it would require the power of a lot of these positives to alleviate our problems so that, confirmed optimists as we were, there could be no meagerly qualifying adjective with loveliness. It must be EVERY LOVELINESS.

These were more than friends who joined us in our dedication. We need a new word to describe the quality of togetherness that develops under the pressures of this century. The search for a more perfect way of life has some likeness to the search for the Grail, itself a symbol. The prosaic and pedestrian effort that goes into the householding and financing of such an adventure has its struggles reminiscent of jousts and bouts, but somehow the arms we used were our heads; and the warfare was weaponless.

Anne Henning from whom things spiritual and well-nigh miraculous came to be, was with us that evening and blessed our project. Mable Miller, whose labors with the youth of north Detroit are embedded in the lives of hundreds of people no longer the sixteen- and seventeen-year-olds she served in those depression days, was also with us. Her memory stays with the place and lives in our work as her white lilac stretches itself above the other lilacs in the hedge. Dr. Edith Swift, copartner dedicated to youth and for half a century in the forefront of every forward movement—suffrage, women in medicine, education in sex, and family living—gave herself to the venture. Her strong arm and clear head, her vision, and her finances had brought the dream to actuality.

These three are no longer with us in body. Anne faded quickly. Mable succumbed to a terrible sickness borne with fortitude. Edith left us in April of 1950 after a long illness.

Those of us still here are Mrs. Eric Gates, then director of YWCA of Detroit and now retired; Misses Edna[1] and Leila White, formerly of Merrill-Palmer School, and myself. Each continues her interest in the general wellbeing of the world and in the things which primarily concern children and their parents.

In the first years we undertook to bring the best brains we could find to think with us week ends and at Sunday teas. Clubs came from one hundred miles away to lunch or dinner with us and listened to or with us afterward as books were reviewed and major topics of interest and importance were discussed. The *Detroit News* called us a "Retreat for Thinkers."

[1] Since died.

Mable's youth groups came to discuss religion as they felt it concerned them. Mrs. Lenz came to discuss and demonstrate flower arrangements. William Norton spoke on social problems. Clarence Hilberry spoke of literature and poetry. Year in and out we pursued these discussions, taking on more and more of them ourselves. We had luncheons for fifty to one hundred women and whoever did not have to speak washed the dishes.

Successful as these affairs had been we still felt that our original problem was unsolved. Many people claimed benefit but these were adults, all carriers of heavy responsibilities. The leadership for the future was still chance and we were not touching it in any real way.

Next, life brought us in contact with young adolescents. As though there was a concerted plan outside ourselves, people began to ask us to take their adolescent children for months at a time. New friends rallied to our assistance to help with recreation and training. This, we thought, was what we wished to do. These were younger and could the easier be made alert to human problems and learn to take a share in their solution. We found this more rewarding in that our effort bore visible fruit in young lives focused and dedicated to a better world. Dozens of these came and stayed to finish school. We found ways to help some to college. Many of them still call Rayswift home; several have established their own homes with their own and others' children.

Then came the race riots in Detroit. Jewish mothers were fearful for their children, threatened as they were by the same storm. Would we take their small children until the city became a safer place? I saw that a more concentrated facility could be made available when the total environment could be controlled. Living conditions were as free of hazard as it was possible to make them. In such rural environment a child could be freed to find his own answers to many of his wonders, without the risk to life and limb which was generally present in urban environment. I saw for myself an opportunity for laboratory study.

Gradually the adolescents left us and parents brought younger ones for us to study. Medical friends who had given generously to our earlier afternoon and week-end meetings began to take an interest in this program. They asked us to take patients who, they felt, needed to be free of overindulgent or oversolicitous parents. Parents brought us children whose above average mental equipment made the city seem a poor environment. We had as many as twenty-five at a time housed inadequately for the year round but satisfactorily for summer. Each parent professed satisfaction with his child's growth, but knew we were only scratching the surface of what could be done.

Finally, with much consultation and planning with experienced camp operators and helpful state officials, we came upon our present organization as a nonprofit corporation under Michigan law, authorized for year-round care of twelve children, ages from three to eighteen. A year later we were permitted by the federal government to publish that gifts were tax exempt. That was in 1944.

Our facilities have been improved since Dr. Swift and I gave our property and equipment to bring Rayswift into being. We own three residences and rent another. We have a staff of five with part-time specialists. Children's fees scaled to necessity furnish 65 per cent of operating costs. Gifts including my own make up the deficit and provide for an occasional addition to capital equipment. We have a long waiting list from all over the nation and thanks to the kindly cooperation of doctors and educators we are able to do some good work with children.

The present board of directors, which differs little from the first one, is made up of the following medical people: Catherine Corbeille; Robert Drews; J. C. Engel, Otto Grob; C. J. Marinus; J. C. Moloney. The educational directors are: Russell Broadhead; Earl C. Kelley; Dorothy LaSalle; Harriet Petry; J. W. Menge; Margaret Sterne. These people have given richly of their experience, time, and money. Mr. Paul Mabley, attorney and agent in residence, Mrs. Bertha E. Waite, the treasurer, and myself have donated our services.

These efforts should not go unrecorded. We have learned a great deal through the years concerning the education of exceptional children. This we have wished to make available to public school teachers pursuant to the stated purposes in our articles of incorporation. It is also our personal purpose to complete the service we have undertaken to render here. The completed report leaves us with a sense of a job done, and curiosity as to whether life will provide other workers and money to pay them so that this job can go on. Next steps are clearly indicated and they need to be taken for the wellbeing of other children who will be directly or indirectly served by us.

The nature of this report cannot but be colored by the eyes of those who have seen it. Lawrence K. Frank has contributed greatly to its general form, and its specific unfolding. His original advice was: state your assumptions and hypotheses and describe what you have seen occur. This prescription is disarmingly simple. We found fairly early that what we thought to be our assumptions were arrived at en route. Such beginning assumptions were more in the nature of axioms which for us seemed beyond the need to question further. We discovered that these were largely below conscious level, and such as would have been stated with an "of course" to introduce them.

What we are now finding basic to our thinking are verifications of some of those earlier unconscious premises, but most often wide modifications of these, as the attempt to state them required a most careful scrutiny of our most fundamental knowledge. These concepts we have tried to state, together with all the machinery by which we came by them in full view, so that to the extent to which such things are possible the reader might experience vicariously what was ours directly. The development of the children—about sixty—who have Rayswift in their vitals is a matter of history in process. How this process came to take the shape it has is of course not wholly within our ken. We have tried to be meticulous in labeling what we knew from what we guessed.

"The knowledge of the 'whole organization' of what occurs in the organism is knowledge of a *unique* kind, which cannot be made superfluous or be replaced by the ascertaining of any causal connections."—ERNST CASSIRER

MARIE I. RASEY

WHAT WE LEARN
FROM CHILDREN

CHAPTER I

We Revise Our Assumptions

The organism over any length of time is essentially a coming and going between different parts. This interchange is what keeps it all together as a unit and spreads it out into its environment. The organism is the way it behaves, and it behaves as a whole.
—A. D. Ritchie: *Natural History of Mind* (p. 184)

1.

Modern biologists point out that structures or forms are the results of processes. A structure is an "after the fact" phenomenon. One may learn a good deal about building a house by building one, but what one learns will not affect the structure of that house. The things he learns will show up only if and when he builds another. When the structure is visible, it is, for that form, beyond the alterations that process can bring. Further modification of structure will require new process. Since process is more difficult to observe than its consequent structures, investigators have a tendency to look where the seeing is good rather than where the seen thing is in the making. This error is peculiarly easy to make in dealing with educational theory since both process and structure are so complex.

We were plagued with this problem also, for we were concerned primarily with growth, which is a complex process and hierarchy of processes. Yet the structures in concepts, life-patterns, and self-images become much easier to identify and observe after they are formed. The attempt to keep our eyes on process and yet demonstrate for the reader what we saw presented a difficult task.

1

As is our general approach we began to *do,* finding that an examination of our own doing could most readily yield us analyzable data. Thus we looked for our basic assumptions in our own ways of observation and interpretation. Some amazing experiences resulted which must be reported by way of introduction.

We discovered that our own beginning assumptions, even in the selection of children, in the establishment of the environing things, people, and experiences, stemmed primarily from deeplying concepts. In fact, they lay largely below consciousness. They were, in a manner of speaking, structures laid down and built up by early experience and by concepts received uncritically from current practice and habituated patterns.

For example, the concepts which lay at the bottom of the Ray-swift venture were of such a kind as: growing children are educable; the whole personality is more than the sum of its parts; a family situation is the optimum circumstance for growth; young feet on soil are in better growth condition than young feet on concrete—the country is more growth-rich than the city. Such assumptions had the nature of axioms.

We discovered as we brought these into conscious consideration that there might be wide difference of opinion about how axiomatic they were. Axiom connotes what is true for every one always. They might, we decided, be axiomatic for us, with no such claim upon others.

Also, neither we nor apparently anyone else had much interest in what assumptions we began with. We were concerned with the growing edge of our assumptions, since it was from this that the changing action patterns we employed seemed to stem. This continuous flux of concepts seemed of a piece with the *process* characteristics in all else we knew about.

Values appear to derive from experience, and in turn these derived values modify action. These actions again yield values, and modify subsequent actions which in their turn modify the always-triggering values as the continuing feedback appears to alter them.

We asked ourselves why a basic assumption operated upon uncritically over long periods of time rises, at some crisis, into consciousness. We had to satisfy ourselves with the answer that, in fact, it did; concepts of an axiomatic nature rose to challenge in moments not apparently crucial enough to establish their inadequacy. As Carrel[1] once helpfully suggested: one case does not establish a law, but it does establish that there is a law governing it, if we can penetrate deeply enough to find it. We decided to rest our present procedure upon the fact that assumptions did come under challenge; and apparently this occurred when in some fashion the assumption did not satisfy the observation.

2.

Small Nancy was chasing a butterfly. Around the corner she came, body poised in a headlong fashion, almost in defiance of gravity. Arms extended upward. Fingers spread in a ready-to-grab half-sphere. Facial muscles were drawn into an expression of expectant success. Lips were slightly parted, eyes round with wonder. All these nicely designed and executed actions rested on assumptions we may need to challenge later.

Now the warm air currents where the summer sun fell full on the greenhouse roof lifted the airborne butterfly beyond the competence of the earth-borne creature to follow. With great accuracy Nancy assessed the situation for which only four years of living had given her judgments. The butterfly, she understood, was beyond her reach.

With a skill not possessed by all problem solvers, she knew when the improbable became the impossible, and when further effort was futile. She was able to alter purpose without emotional waste. The small feet changed direction with almost imperceptible change of speed. She slid down on the dry grass beside me, trying to catch more elusive things than butterflies.

"What are you doing?" I inquired.

"I'm catching a butterfly," Nancy answered.

Concerned as I was to see how and what I was thinking, I became alert. Why, I asked myself, does this description seem inaccurate to me? Did an over-optimistic child take the intent for the deed? Had her present experience no need for a more accurate term? Was this necessity of mine no necessity of hers?

[1] Alexis Carrel, *Man the Unknown* (New York: Harper & Brothers, 1939).

I concluded that my reality was more demanding than hers. I had pursued so much beside butterflies which I had not caught that my reality demanded another term to describe it. Was this possibly a reason that we had believed that "out of the mouths of babes" came wisdom, when what actually came was a simplified statement of fact unencumbered by the excess baggage with which experience often loads us? It appeared that the more experience one had, the more words he required to convey it. Merely more words were not enough. Nuances in experience demanded nuances in terms as well. If these observations were valid, they rendered rather senseless our usual school procedure of giving children masses of others' experience to read about as a means to a large vocabulary.

Nancy broke in upon my reverie with a comment that made this day memorable in my own intellectual growth.

"Now I know," she cried, in the voice of one who has found a jewel, "why butterfly nets have long handles!"

This statement might not have been astounding had it not been that our household boasted no butterfly net. The only place where she might have experienced one lay miles away and a quarter of her life in the past. That experience must have been question-laden to have remained till now, but it had never showed up demanding an answer, though other things had. "The dead past" had apparently not "buried its dead." In fact, the past was still much alive. How? The sweep of action, or of her "ongoingness," had sucked up into its stream an item out of a past we had always thought to be fixed and finished, and made it present again! Could it be that these past events were no more static than anything else? That seemingly bankrupt venture with long-handled nets involved itself in a moving current, and not only did this new learning profit, but the old came out of bankruptcy solvent again!

Also, there seemed something wrong about the "again." If we can keep these has-beens in some manner of flux—and it seems likely that nothing need be done about the keeping except to recognize it—all that we have experienced is ours forever. The ongoingness of experience, the process of growth, may flow through pleasant lands or waste. The flow is the thing. This thinking opens up questions. Let us examine Nancy's action further.

It is possible for the observer to communicate his experience superficially by saying: "Small Nancy came running," but no one can conceive of stating adequately all that is implicit in this simple action.

She came into view, balanced, arms outstretched, lips parted. One saw actually an ordinary occurrence in which a four-year-old ran. Yet this running was a fragment of process in her day, one instant in a four-year span. That small proportion would grow even smaller as day succeeded day, and year succeeded year. This process relates only to Nancy. And before Nancy was herself? Manifestly she was two organisms. Still earlier, four and as time dwindled and dimmed in its long past, her share as Nancy became small beyond description. Is it for each of us also a truth that "before Abraham was, I am"?

The single individual organism becomes less than the dust when we see one lifetime against the backdrop of all who live and have lived. Yet by the same token, this observation raises the short span of that single organism, without which the chain is broken, to gigantic proportion. Will ongoingness proceed through her, as she may give the body she is to procreation, or by other mechanism reproduce whatever kind she may prove to be as thinker, actor, artist, in arts and in artistic living? The strands in the braid of life are many and various. To get a glimpse of its total continuity will require sharper thinking.

That fine balance, which was already an accomplished skill, reduced to habitual and reflexive patterns with the scant three of her four years of conscious memory, had "elsewhere its beginning, and cometh from afar." It seems to be present in the early days of the human animal's existence. Long before feet can manage standing or great muscles of the legs and torso are available for locomotion, the urge to stand erect makes itself evident when small feet press the mother's hip or thigh when the child is picked up. Some months later, what looks like wonder or curiosity makes a traveler of this child. All four limbs appear to recall tissue-old skills in makeshift locomotion. He crawls or creeps. He becomes adept at covering ground, but something more recent triggers the tissue's or the personality's purposes.

He forgoes his well-developed all-four locomotion. He permits himself to be inept or ineffective in two-legged going. Superficially we say, "The baby is learning to walk." Actually he has given a fresh evidence of his share or place in the procession of ongoingness. From here on he becomes increasingly adept as a walking organism. When his peers wish to label him in the highest reaches of the ethical values to which he may aspire, they will use the same term with which we describe his first faltering attempts to adapt himself to gravity. They will call him an upright man.

Nancy also manifests a link in the procession. All this running is to fulfill a purpose which may have been uniquely hers, but may also have been the echo of earlier experience when small moving objects were pursued and caught, for reasons long forgotten, in still persistent sequences. These called for unique team work between muscles which had to be fed sugar to burn for the extra effort. Endocrines had to countersign the order before it could be cashed at the sugar bank. Extra sugar delivery placed new demands upon the delivery mechanism. Waste-laden blood had to be purified and relieved of its burden with an increased respiration. "The organism is the way it behaves, and it behaves as a whole." To do all this, human tissue has to have its environing sea upon which sail its corpuscles at a mean temperature which does not exist in our prone reptilian forebears. For them it is too warm. It differs also from that maintained by the bird people, also somehow related to us far down the family tree. For them it would be too cold. Uniquely fit as an internal environment, it puts our human specimen into the right thermodynamics for its unique purposes.

Thus it seemed to us that our assumptions of an active growing child had been too superficially conceived. This small human is a carrier of ongoingness in greater and at the same time simpler fashions than our heedless assumptions had included. Her growth is interrelated with all life.

Thus our simple concept of children growing up brings us a new sense of the worth of the individual. We may not be satisfied with our forebears' statement that all men are created free and equal. The daring pronouncements about equality may be more complex than their proponents thought them to be, since there are so many aspects of life in which to attempt equality. We may see freedom as a skill to develop rather than a right inherited. But we shall see that each person is equally precious to life and that life embodies more than we once guessed.

3.

When, according to Genesis, light had been separated from darkness, fluid from solid, and first living plants created, the next day's task had to be of quite another kind. Fish and fowl and beast and other growing creatures had to wait until sun and moon had been created, stars given their appointed places, and time provided in which the growers could grow. Time, it appears, is of the essence.

Returning again to Nancy and her butterfly business, we find we must reconsider the item of time. Glib phrases with which we have packaged and labeled our ignorances have been misleading. For example; this whole observation of Nancy in pursuit exists in what we have called the past. It is experience both for her and for us who observed it. Each of us sees out from within it (*ex-perio*) as through a window. It occurred in what we called present. It was geared to serve what was then the future, all three of which are now fused in what we loosely define as the past. When we undertake to define these more closely for practical purposes of observation and recording, the concepts begin to move into areas of metaphysics, perhaps bordering on the mystic and religious.

Nancy desired to be where she was not, namely where the butterfly was. Quite literally she "took steps" to that end. She took them as apparently all physical phenomena must occur at some intersection of here and now—a moving point, which can no longer be defined as present. No chronometer is fine enough to split those seconds, although a quick action camera can come as close to it as the speed of light permits. Nonetheless the lifted foot for the next step presupposes space upon which to land it and time for the landing. Both concepts lie in the not-yet, and the about-to-be is an act of faith. It is indeed "the substance of things hoped for." The hope is justified. The faith is made manifest. The step is taken. We could then satisfy the demands of the moving growth through, or perhaps in, time had we only its linear aspect to conjure with. We would raise both the not-yet and the has-been to such dimensions that both past and future were conceived as the present, not as a period, but as a dividing tissue between the two. Time's flow could be channeled through an aperture in that tissue. The shape of that aperture would determine the form the energy took as it passed through. The halt that we postulate is for our own convenience. There is no halt in the flow of time. The halt is in the consciousness of the observer.

When, however, one gets a glimpse of how many presents it takes to make a past, how many yesterdays are implicit in today, and how many beams from how many various angles have come to focus in any particular now, the whole multi-dimensionality intrudes on the issue, "It behaves as a whole."

This internal complexity includes the yesterdays, more likely yester-aeons, in which open-ended tubes got themselves involved and became digestive tract. It includes the internal negative electric charge, and the surface positive charge which so neatly keeps apart corpuscular bodies in midstream; it includes the necessity to overcome this separateness with cell cement, when cells involve themselves in tissue-building. Nerve, muscle, nutriating, eliminating systems, endocrine-thalamus, smooth muscle, cortical-striated muscle—all separate, all together—"behave as a whole." They are described in "Nancy took steps." It began with an act of faith and ended in the act of chemistry; or it began in chemistry and came back to chemistry, depending upon where in the process one cuts in to look.

The process is even more complex than it appears. It is also the product of ages during which the learnings of tissue and colloid, nerve-fibre and muscle, were laid down in the organism until the processes were resolved into highly automatized sequences. Food partly digested passes through the pylorus to its further digesting and no amount of "taking thought" can let one sense its happening. Neither command nor negation alters the flow of endocrine which in turn releases the stored sugar. For better or worse these are set beyond the interference of consciousness. This fact appears to be one of growth economy. It leaves consciousness unencumbered except at the epiphyses of our growing, where the in-building is in process and values can be weighed in terms of the purposes they serve.

It is small wonder in all this welter that finite mind found its first explanation by raising its own knowings, aspirations, expectation to the power of infinite, put a capital letter to fit the infinite, and then waged wars and nurtured prejudices in terms of how we should call him, or Him, according to one's preference. In our present allergy to the anthropomorphic, we depersonalize, take away the Middle Ages' concept of great shoulders and flowing beard, and in the newer editions, replace the term "God" with the capitalized term "The Eternal." To practical-minded individuals, that is people who are intent upon practicing their profession of being human, the name that is named seems less crucial than appreciating the dynamics which give some degree of control of the practice.

The practicer observes that he takes the stuff of the not-yet, acts his faith upon it, and things of his own contriving come to pass. He may also observe that in spite of his best contriving what he plans does not come to pass, and in its place comes another and better effect than he had visioned. Is the contriver inept? Is life adept? One concept has evolved to us from these questions that brings forth more of their kind, rather than answers. This accrues from looking steadfastly at the process and only slightly at the structure. We see that things we design and things we do not design come to pass, out of the tomorrows of all of us into our todays. Come to pass they do, but to see the creating process we must punctuate differently. The significance lies in the comma. They come, to pass.

Long ago we recognized in other areas that our over-all economy on earth demanded that we die as well as live. We understand that only successive passages of generation after generation of grain and flower and fruit, and flock after flock, and herd after herd, and society after society hold the possibility of the better and best. Passing into other manifestation becomes as essential to growth in both short- and long-span growths. To come is to pass. And to pass is also to come!

How shall coming and passing be achieved except as time is

seen as of the essence? Stature has to be waited for as well as fed for. Learning, so much of it skill and requiring repeated experiencing, takes time. "All becoming, though there is no other way of being, takes time," says Gabriel.[2] The recognition of the time it takes, we have learned, minimizes the sense of hurry, the tension so frequent when we undertake to abet nature with nurture. We do not find it difficult to be patient for tulips' bloom when we plant tulip bulbs. "In their good time," we say. We anticipate May, but we do not expect to produce it in December. Once accepting the assumption that tulips take time to achieve their ten days' flowering, and children their varying time indices for their longer flowering, the nurturer has no further need for the much overrated virtue of patience. It is simply not relevant. Time is of the essence. It comes, to pass.

As corollary we also assume that the passing need not require emotional expenditures. The baby in its crib does not know the hazards of a slippery floor which he will one day have to walk. The mother may be anxious that she does not drop him when his locomotion depends on her. But that he drops himself, when he has forsaken forever lying prone as a way of life and has become a walker, she accepts. There are new hazards. They also pass. Security on both feet and then on one foot after the other will come, and will pass too, and the shuffling part will come, and pass into a longer lying prone.

Teachers can know that the wide-eyed wonderers of the early grades will come to be serious pursuers of their wonders. Midway of the process they may need to poke and punch all and sundry for no better reason than to see where they themselves leave off and others begin. And even this passes and there comes a self-consciousness which often makes the teacher wish for the old pushy days as a mother may often wish her child out of his questions and back in his quiescent crib.

The ongoingness has come from remote eras. Out of the always fecund dark has come light. Solid substance divides from fluids. Animate differs from inanimates. The youngest and the most unable as well as the oldest and most able, and all that is in

[2] Gerald Heard, *Gabriel and the Creatures* (New York: Harper & Brothers, 1952).

between are part and parcel of the ongoingness of life. The ongoing for species as well as for specimen takes time. The going is as essential to the wave as its coming. Its systole demands its diastole.

4.

One of the most valued fruits of ongoingness in time and action is experience. "It is a good school"; "it is an expensive school"; "only fools learn there"—are proverbial expressions of the value human kind sets on the fruits of doing and of thinking upon that doing. Learning by experience is a statement of a philosophy of education as it is the core of religions of long history. It may well be that both of the terms, learning and experience, will bear further scrutiny.

Learning is in our language a present participle which serves both to describe activity in process, as "he is learning to skate," and as a substantive noun, as in "a little learning." This double usage confuses our thinking. We shall discard this latter meaning for our purposes, and mean by learning that in-the-process state in which incompleteness is implicit. Implicit also is the concept of using and doing. "Do you knit?" one may inquire, and understand by the answer, "I'm learning," that this is not the person from whom to order a pair of socks in the argyle manner.

If the person addressed studies a book on the history of knitting, the uses to which the skill is put, but uses her hands for no other purpose than to turn the pages, we agree that she is not learning to knit. She may be learning about it. This distinction is not always recognized.

Much confusion results, for example, when people assume they are teaching religion by having children occupy themselves with making models of the temple or mapping the journey of St. Paul. These activities, praiseworthy for stimulating children's interest in things *about* religion and for engaging them in a degree of activity, are essential to learning. They are nonetheless *about* religion. They are not in themselves religious experiences. They may rank higher as tools for learning about religion than the memorizing of verses or the ability to recite the names of the books of the Bible. They will however never suffice to teach religion as a way of life which like other skills will have to be learned by doing.

We mean by "learning," the acquiring of a skill or knowledge or attitude to the extent that we have the ability to use the new item. We know what we can do, but until we can do something with it, we do not know.

Experience connotes doing. What has been experienced has been done, but the reverse seems not too true. Not all things done appear to leave a residue of experience behind them. It may turn out that this residue has different degrees of volatility. Attitudes may be of so high a fusion quality that, like salt in a soup, the whole is permeated by the new addition. Repetitive doing lays down its residue in intricate constellations of nerve-muscle coordination, so that thousands of miles of doing in the matter of driving a car adds little to one's conscious knowledge, but adds greatly to one's skill. The fruit of experience on the more cumbersome knowledge level may merely add another item to a cumulating mass of knowledge, or it may furnish the final completing item which makes of what was merely an accumulation, an entity, an emergent. It is something new, differing often in properties and characteristics from those of its component parts.

As we look closely at the process by which experience appears to result, we notice that experience is a structure built up from the results of the processes which preceded it. It is related to the effectiveness of the action which brought it into being. If we shift focus to the action pattern, we must ask ourselves, what acts? What makes the action action? The physicists will tell us that where there is action we may infer energy release. Energy release requires going one step further back. We must ask what triggers that release? The answer, should we find it, will lie still further back in a dim area labeled value-judgments by many. And whence comes the value-judgment? Why do we require a hyphen? This one we can answer. Judgment has to do with the choice of pattern of action by the actor, and choice implies some preference among patterns. Because in actuality one outweighs the other and the weightier tips the scale, we require the ingredient of value to describe our process.

The persistent questioner must still inquire, whence came the values? The obvious answer is: from experience. Now we have come full circle. The parent wishes for his child what he himself learned by experience. Often the parent wishes to get this value for his child without the effort, time, and often pain incident to much experiencing. That was what school was about. Life would have taught him ultimately, if painfully and slowly. School was a way to short-cut experience. What has been accomplished is that all know more than they did about the process, learning. We know something of its sequences. We know something of a climate favorable to its culture. But a substitute for experience we do not have.

A specific experience cannot in the nature of things come back full circle. Circumstances in which experience moves are changing. It is for this reason that recurring similar experiencing can improve the quality of one's doing. New has been added. One learns to be skillful with a golf club or with comforting the sick. "Practice" can make, but does not guarantee, "perfect."

Another aspect of experience challenges our attention. Things do happen for the first time both to specimen and species. There was a time in the life of each of us when we had not gone to school. That experience was formless in the not-yet. Yet the firstness of it is misleading. Before it took shape in a present moment, it existed as dream, wish, intent, purpose. Above the falls the waters seem sluggish. They appear to gather momentum as they approach the fall and seem to hurl themselves downward with intent. Beginning to go to school may be a dread or dream in the thought of the mother. It may gain a pallid reflection in the young child's consciousness. It may gather momentum from a knowledge of others' experience, but it waits its own unique time to take shape in some present.

This inadequate example is an attempt to express those intensifying factors which pull or push some not-yet event through the shaping present, and it *is*. It is here that the shapelessness takes shape. Shaped, it emerges as experience. This is repetitive in statement, but so is the process. Its process demands a roadbed upon which to travel. It structures it as surely as pulsing blood structures a new path around an embolism. The process appears to be one, but the structures it creates are many and on many levels of manifestation.

As we have followed our process in reverse we have set up a

sequence which we state as: experience—value-judgment—purpose—energy—release—action—experience. This second experience triggers the whole process again and again. We came all this way when we undertook to discover what we meant when we voiced as a purpose of our own: "I am going to observe this child." We saw how much easier it was to look at the child as a structure than at his ongoingness as a process. The analysis of the process finally wound up in an abbreviation of the above-stated sequence.

We now say, when we propose to observe a child, we will look backwards over the sequence in that section of ongoingness where he now is, and ask: how effective is this organism in achieving his ends? Was the action appropriate? How was the quality and quantity of the energy he had or made available to the purposes he appeared to have judged valuable to his ends? Energy—action —effect is a sequence which is verifiable. Value-judgement—purpose we are assuming as preceding it. These lie at this time beyond all but inference. We recognize the assumption as such and use the terms "value-judgment" and "purpose" to describe what we assume occurs. The one subsumes all we think goes on when all the knowing and feeling of species and specimen are somehow coordinated as measures of weight which are employed as basis for the second, the casting of the die, the process of choice.

Sometimes in the summer months our young people make a job of fixing bouquets for their table. To be chosen as the fixer by one's table mates is construed as a worthwhile distinction. The child chosen finds from his adults what vase he may have and then he finds from the wild flowers and the gardens what flowers he would like to pick. There are no prohibitions upon the field flowers except that they are not to be picked in excessive quantities and let die. It is necessary to ask adults if one picks in the gardens. This serves the purposes of learning to consult, knowing how some flowers are valued over others, and why some are "saved for seed." The project also gives excellent scope for observation of purpose-effectiveness as well.

It was late August. Wild asters and sunflowers filled the fields and blossomed in the flower beds. Observers were about in inconspicuous roles. I came upon small Heidi. She was sitting on the near side of what had been the brook but now was a desultory trickle. The grass on the banks was brown and dry as well, but on the far side, back, perhaps twenty feet away from her, there stood a large clump of deep purple wild asters. Heidi was hunched up with her arms clasped about her still bony knees. "Are you fixing flowers for your table?" I inquired. She nodded yes. English was still an uneasy way of communication, and the native German was no longer as available as it had been.

"Were you planning to get those flowers?" I inquired.

She was quiet so long I glanced at her to see if she had understood. Her face muscles were working in a masterful effort to get the words out.

"It is too far enough and too hard enough," was her understandable rejoinder. I was debating whether this was the time to satisfy the child's expressed need, serving my own ego well but perhaps serving the child badly, or whether I should do the difficult and unromantic job of waiting to see what she could make of her difficulty. Then we were aware of Don who had come upon us and halted beside me. He had a pair of clippers in his hand, and the beaten-down grass around the clump became understandable.

"Are you going to get those flowers?" he inquired.

"We thought we might, but Heidi thinks it is too hard and too far. So I guess we won't. Are you after them?"

"Yes. I was here once and they were too tough, so I went back and got these," showing the clippers. "Are you tired, Heidi?" he asked.

It passed through my thought that this was a queer question, one child to another. But it was not queer. It was consistent. He was trying to understand what could keep two people from getting what they wanted when all that stood between them and their desire was twenty feet of space. He had to find the answer, as do we all, out of his own knowledge. All that he knew which could have hindered him would have been fatigue. Heidi had indicated that she was not tired and so had I. Then Don was driven to classify us with the only label his experience had to offer.

"Sissies," he said.

We accepted the label without any belief in it because I, at least, knew that neither he nor I, nor anyone else, could see another except through his own eyes. It has to do with how one understands himself, the perception or image he has of himself. We knew that however much one trained himself in so-called objectivity, these eyes and these yesterdays combined would determine what each one's eyes saw, or as has been succinctly stated: "What we know comes from us."[3] Thus one learns that to be called sissy, or rascal, or dullard, does not make that a fact. It is not so much a judgment made by the observer upon another as it is a revelation of the observer's way of looking.

I asked Don another question. He was not one to make the effort to come back a second time. He was much more likely to call something an impossibility and be satisfied with one try. I said: "How come you came all the way back a second time? There were plenty of purple flowers in the bed by the drive."

The look he flashed at me was one of bafflement that one who had answered for him so many questions he considered difficult should ask such a foolish one now. In that instant I came to know what made a question a foolish question. It is just that the questioned knows the answer, and so for him, of course, it *is* foolish.

"I came back after these because these were the ones I wanted."

Walking about I came on Gerald. He was sitting in the sand box, running sand from one hand to the other. Poor Gerald—he and sand! Shifting sand has always been our symbol for ineffectiveness. He was our symbol. He was a puzzle in that he registered high in I. Q. and was able in body. Someone volunteered that Gerald had been chosen by his table to gather a bouquet.

"Is that right?" I said. "What are you going to do?"

"I didn't know what vase, and I thought those pink ones, maybe, but I didn't know if I could pick them."

"Would you like to try? I could find you a vase," I offered tentatively.

"No, I guess not. Nothing I try to do comes out, anyway." It was an accurate observation on his part.

"If you want to do it, I will help."

[3] E. C. Kelley, *Education for What Is Real* (New York: Harper & Brothers, 1947).

"No, I guess not. I guess I'll stay here and finish my fort."

"Where is your fort?"

"I haven't begun it yet. I'm just doing this," and another handful of sand dripped back into the box. Heidi had judged the flowers she wanted as too hard to get and too far away, which is a way of saying I do not have fuel enough to make action effective, and not even enough to espouse a purpose.

Gerald had energy enough but his desires were unfocused into any purpose. The focus lack may have been an actual outcome of failures, and it may have been imaginary. For all practical purposes it makes no real difference whether his judgment of his performance is valid in external fact or not. It is the value he holds and the judgment he makes that trigger the release of energy into action or clamp shut to hold back energy. We might prefer a different terminology than the poets. Actually the substance is truth. "There is nothing either good or bad, but thinking makes it so."

If, as it appeared to us, value-judgments are so crucial to action, we needed to look over our thinking in this area and to define our terminology. The literature on value-judgments is voluminous. The practical thinking is less available. If we look for the source of these values, we can find them on at least three levels and emanating from three sources. There appear to be "values" which are resident in tissue which never reach consciousness in the course of their use (Sherrington). The blinking eye, the involuntary movement of the head when flying objects are perceived hint at judgments deriving from aeons of experience, which may have been conscious at some earlier time, or may be as deep and as elemental as the intricately triggered endocrine, thalamic, smooth-muscle sequences which automatize the internal maintenance system of the specimen and the species.

A second level of values seems to be those which have dropped out of consciousness as reasoned responses. They appear to be reduced for body economy reasons to the habit level. The organism tends to act as it has been acting. This only means that more or less remotely these habitual responses in judgment were associated with learned values, learned either by specimen

in this unique organization or learned by the species and built into the automatic response system.

Dorsey records an interesting example in *Why We Behave Like Human Beings*.[4] He had returned to his boyhood farm home for a summer devoted to writing. His study was on the second floor. At two-thirty of the morning when he had put the last penstroke to his task, he decided to tiptoe down the back stairs and get a drink before retiring. He did not turn on the light. As he crossed the kitchen in getting to the sink he ducked his head, as he later realized to avoid a pump handle which had not been there for thirty years, when his head had occupied space approximately two feet nearer the floor. Such persistent response patterns which lie in such profusion in the yesterdays of all of us rise to protect or plague us when new occasions require new judgments to solve the problems they present.

A third level of value-judgment appears to be employed in those areas in which no judgment so far arrived at has been repeated sufficiently to habitualize it. The weighing of worths is carried on in consciousness and the organism appears to arrive at the decision stage wholly by reason processes. Yet every observer has noted that arguments which carry conviction to the person verbalizing them are often revealing to a listener who cannot understand how the verbalizer can miss his own evident discrepancies. Adler taught that one often found the real validation not in the first or second argument offered, but behind such verbal flags as "and besides" where the true value usually lurks.

An irate teacher whose nerves had been worn out trying to help a child whose pampered self-centeredness was most trying, sent for the child's mother. When she came, on the defensive, the jangling nerves got further irritation as might have been expected. The teacher proceeded with what we describe as "telling off."

As the teacher's wrath was fanned by her own talk as well as the heated responses of the mother, the teacher forsook the diplomacy she had been taught. She grew more and more

[4] George A. Dorsey, *Why We Behave Like Human Beings* (New York: Harper & Brothers, 1926).

uncontrolled—a picture which she did not usually show and which she had been at some effort to master. Hours later in discussing the episode, she said: "John is a complete nuisance. He hinders the other children, and besides I just can't stand fat women who wear outsize pink dresses." A large book could be written of such telltale phrases which mask emotional blow-up.

In those many trying, soul-rending situations the individual who undertakes to lead his life toward ideals he visualizes must be able to protect his judgments to the degree that he can recognize and control the pervasive emotional elements in the situation. When through the years a person behaves most frequently on the controlled side, he comes to be called an understanding soul. Less able people seek his kind as advisers or even just as listening posts, while the disturbed one drains off in speech his internal excess. It may also be said of such: he has good judgment. The latter statement, when true, merely says that this individual has weighed his values both rational and nonrational in such fashion that they have furthered constructive ends for himself and others. Such judgments have been made with sufficient frequency as to establish them as ways of living—life patterns. Since judgment, like many such abstractions, exists rather as an exercised skill than as a quantum of commodity, it is the "practice which makes perfect" or at least which moves toward perfection.

Whether our definition of value-judgment agrees with that of others is unimportant. It has served its purpose if it defines what we are striving to observe and nurture in those areas or processes in which the judgment that some goal merits paying for in some coin is transmuted into goal-directed action.

By whatever name these triggerings are called, they constitute the crucial aspect of ongoingness. Skill in making judgments, skill in selecting from among values that are calculated to serve one's over-all goals is the distinguishing mark between slave and free. Fine judgment can develop from crude judgments only as the judger has recognition of fine nuances in values. The most logical concomitant of this assumption is that any facility calculated to further education will be bound to afford opportunity for learning by experiencing values, which in the best understanding of the nurturer can be expected to yield the values thought consistent with the unique qualities and characteristics of the species homo, more rather than less sapiens.

Learning then would seem more profitable in the midst of living than set apart from it. "Knowing about" could then more readily be distinguished from the more potent "knowing" that results from being involved in rather than told about the process.

We ask ourselves continuously, "But what is the mechanism by which we come by values?" Latterly we have changed the labels. We do not talk any more about push buttons which start mental and emotional processes going. Push buttons are too static, and the intervention of a new force, the pusher, is disturbing. Instead the physicists teach us to use their term "trigger" out of the relay concept. The sight of the luscious fruit triggers the saliva's flow; the mastication triggers the swallowing consummation and so on to the rejection of the unused.

In a comparable parallelism, the sight of lines on a printed page may trigger memories of experience which in turn will trigger the writing hand to compose a letter to reunite lives separated by bitterness and hate. The values, it appears, are the triggering thing. They appear, to use another physicist's term, to come into consciousness as feedback not alone to single processes, but as though each represented a strand in a braid which gave continuous inventory on many levels at once.

But we must not be betrayed by the intricacies of the processes inside the "skin-limited" self, for this is at once all of self there is and a small portion of it. It is a self-contained process so far as the energy is released or withheld from acting, but all such withholding or spending is inexorably related to all else which is comprised in the "not-self" or environment. For several reasons we have preferred Ames' less equivocal term, "externality." All that is not at any given instant inside the skin is outside, yet the correspondence between externality and internality is of the type of respiration and of ingestion of liquid and solids. As Angyal[5] has pointed out, a plate of food set before one is environmental. When it is eaten it promptly becomes organismal. Diastole and systole show again. We cannot leave these internal aspects of values without seeing by what process and mechanics these values are modified by the inter-relation of the organism with its externality of things and people.

[5] Andras Angyal, *Foundations for a Science of Personality* (New York: Commonwealth Fund, 1941).

CHAPTER II

We See the Child in His Environment Differently

Thus a person does not lead a purely individual life, but also a family life, a social life, a cultural life in which he participates and which he shares with others.

—ANDRAS ANGYAL

1.

It is difficult to discuss environment in terms of demonstrable fact, for all those things in externality which are in process of flowing into an organism operate on so many levels of intake, and so much of the mechanics must be considered a matter of assumption since it lies outside present laboratory procedures.

The painting of a lone farmhouse amid bare trees with an icebound brook on the one side and a snow-drifted fence on the other flows into consciousness on the levels of color, form, composition, as well as the mood-colored memories it may stir. These two differ again from such inflow as may result from one's personal and social relations with the painter.

Our newer knowledge about perception calls for a rethinking of the whole matter. We have been accustomed to saying that the environment makes individuals what they are. It was easy enough to see that the social or economic or educational matrix in which an individual is set makes its contribution to the shape, form, nature of that individual.

The impact of a piece of music played for the first time for an audience of trained musicians in the paneled music room in

22

one's home falls upon different ears than would be available to a listener whose earlier musical experience was derived from juke box records played by customers in one's family's restaurant.

When, however, we look at individuals, we see that a prior and continuing force must be taken into account. The unique nature of perception makes it evident that the individual first makes his own environment in terms of his selection from all of those items to which he will give attention, weight and value. As these choices, and perhaps even preferences when choices are not available, tend to constellate into value patterns, they take over the making with a vengeance. Then the environment does indeed make. This choosing appears to extend beyond the tangible things and people which constitute externality, and encompass patterns of relating to these items. The individual may tend to look upon or feel toward an item or a person differently than the person nearest to him does. One sees a task as an opportunity; another sees it as a thankless job. These attitudes condition the quality of relationship established.

The girl who sees the task of baby sitting as the essential link between herself and her hire relates to the task differently than she who sees the job as preparation for her later living of which she is going to be part.

The natural environment of peoples contributes to their characteristics. The anthropologists speak of the fiercer qualities of the mountain groups over those of similar blood who are native to plains. Fisher folk appear to develop specialized qualities associated with the changefulness of the sea and the ever-present hazards it presents. Gray misty tracts like the Aleutians and the long-night areas in polar regions make their mark upon the outlook of their peoples. It is the outlook, rather than that which is looked out upon, that determines the values assigned to what is seen.

But there have been mild mannered dreamers from the mountains, and fierce fighters among the plainspeople. Even allowing for the factor of the individual's selection of items within the totality of his concepts, we cannot account for human values by reference to physical environment alone. The most crucial of all externality items are perhaps those persons who compose the human environment.

The human individual feeds upon his fellows. Most of his energy-expenditure is directed toward or for other human beings. As he enhances others, he enhances himself. As he detracts from others, he detracts from himself. And this is true also in reverse.

The human environment is the most crucial environing factor; and the most crucial aspect for humans is the philosophies they operate upon, the constellation of values that trigger their actions.

Helen was a child of thirteen when she came. She had reason to feel rejected by most people. She had been reared by grandparents who had pampered her in an attempt to make up for other rejections. Her love was channeled into devotion to a mangy bird with whose ugliness she made some identification. Grandparents had not been able to keep her in school. We had difficulty with this matter too. However a variety of changed conditions finally gave Helen a little peace, and in the course of weeks she became at home both at Rayswift and at school. The ancient bird died and a kitten took its place and the lessened need reduced the fierceness of the attachment. Years passed and Helen became eager for college. She came of teacher parents and wanted no part of being a teacher, she thought.

Science was difficult, she thought. She would spend herself only on such difficult things as would establish herself in her own eyes at least.

Helen was inclined to do what pleased her whether her goals fell into usual patterns or not. She entered meteorology, made her way brilliantly, was graduated and went to work for the government. At least a year later, I returned to my college office to find Helen sitting waiting. Before I could get my coat off, she was saying:

"Do you think I would make a teacher?"

"Why not," I asked, "but aren't you the one who never wanted to have anything more to do with teachers?"

"Yes, but that isn't the point. I've spent better than a year of my life—a year—with nothing more alive than graphs and tables.

You are to blame for my not being satisfied with the weather," she said accusingly. "I heard and saw so much of working with people when I was at Rayswift that I'm just not satisfied to be working with anything else."

Helen returned to college, took a master's degree in education, and is teaching happily and successfully. If the values-behavior aspect of the human environment is its most crucial factor, then it becomes increasingly important that children be related with adults whose value constellations lie on the side of ongoingness and therefore outgoingness. Those humans whose values appear to be aligned with self-acquisition and getting, turn children in upon themselves to starve to death; whereas to feed they must turn out toward people and spend rather than hoard.

If this assumption proves valid, it gives us pause to consider the significance of those not-quite-real people who speak from radio and gaze out from television screens and movie projectors. Clever dealers of death and snatchers of possessions carry more values more entertainingly than are likely to accrue from the experiences most generally provided for school consumption. We may choose to compete with the dispensers of villain and hoodlum values by becoming as expert as they in the presentation of what we consider more useful values.

At Rayswift with money to spend, as each child has, the movies are seldom attended. Comic books appear only when some unimaginative guest wants to bring a gift. Television is not part of our equipment since none of the adults so far knows how to make wise use of this type of mass medium. Radio carries much of the same fare, but it also is little used except as a noise concomitant. No prohibitions of adults are imposed in any of these areas.

We assume that what one goes by and what one does is critically important to growing children. The problem of enlisting children in activities thus becomes a matter of communication. How do we make and maintain interpersonal relations so that people can share themselves with each other? This problem of give and take between and among individuals is reminiscent of the biological problem which halted so many species. Radiation and absorption require surface in the right proportion to mass.

Those creatures not so geared did not survive. Within the human body cortex convolutions, intestinal coilings, and the bodies in colloids provide a maximum of surface in their spheroid peripheries. A human personality which has a meager mass cannot support many interchange relationships. The rich mass can be hindered from dispensing itself by too little relatedness. The whole problem of communication is tied up with these characteristics of the interrelationships we must make and maintain. The ratio between mass to support and surface to receive and give in the questions of maintenance seems almost duplicated in the so-called "small" personality, with its limited interrelations to support it and provide it with the substance to share, and the so-called "expansive" personality which appears somehow to replenish itself because it spends itself.

Approached from this angle we find once more the human problem of communication. If there must be interpenetration and interflow, by what channels and with what mechanisms can this be accomplished? We find that the necessity to communicate must be accepted as we study the interrelation of our children with each other and with their adults. We must also review our basic assumptions about it.

Heidi, mentioned previously, was just five when she came. Half her brief life had been spent in Germany and her language was German. She had command of about ten English words. Sometimes her confusion of tongues brought her to ask what an object was called in German, and then she spoke her entire sentence thus. Finally—a matter of months—the balance turned in the direction of English with a rare interjection of a German word. For months beyond this, the sentence structure was Teutonic although the sentence might be made entirely of English words.

Theoretically this child should have had great difficulty in communication. Actually she was not entirely dependent upon verbalization with her peer group where experiences were largely the same. It was longer before adults and she established free intercourse. We needed to revise our communications thinking in terms of our observations of Heidi. We began by thinking that her culture pattern had given her different labels for the same objects, actions, and characteristics, and that she would gradually exchange one label in one language for another label in another. We expected a period of confusion and finally the free-flowing use of the new labels. We discovered that this point of view is a great over-simplification, and that what was looked upon as the major task, the use of the strange new labels, was actually a small part of the whole process.

Once she came to inquire, what do we call village in German? "Dorf," I responded. "Oh, yes, houses and stores." Thus a total experience changed label and apparently the process of exchange went back and forth in her mind. These words exchanged were the obvious method of her communication, but by no means the only one.

Physical contact is a method of communication also. It is often overlooked in dealing with children particularly. It may be that, for the young especially, the pressure of encircling arms, a pat on the shoulder, the contact of face to face act as large-order symbols by which the less able and less verbal young organism communicates with the nurturing and more able adult.

We noticed that Heidi made use of inarticulate crying, the only tool of the nonverbal infant, more than other children her age. Her small fingers were always seeking contact with the face or arms of persons near her, by which it appeared she strengthened her sense of security and possibly a oneness with the trusted person.

Dependent people, usually pampered people, cry more than others. We might perhaps assume that the inarticulate cry belongs to early growth stages as does phantasy. Tardily we are recognizing the place of physical contact in the development of nursing babies. Investigations into the psychological aspect of cutaneous excitement, in process in several quarters, are pointing toward specific personality traits and unique behavior on the part of children born by caesarean section rather than squirming their way through the birth canal.

Heidi also operated with what seemed like a sympathetic understanding with other children, especially new ones who came with difficulties of one or another kind. She seemed to recognize more quickly than the rest emotional or physical needs of children and to make correspondence with them. This seldom resulted in verbalized generalizations as was her way in relation to her own progress. It manifested itself in snuggling, comforting techniques, taking by the hand, adjusting stools or chairs, and the like. Here communication was established by the touch but not initiated by it. The first day of her second year in school she came out of the building with a new nine-year-old on each hand. They towered above her though for psychological reasons each of them was less in command of himself than she.

"Did you have to look after the boys?" I inquired.

"Yes," she answered. "They are strangers and I knew they wouldn't know where to go."

How did she know? They had not asked for help, yet they did need it. And why is it that children, dogs and cats, and horses, and certain childlike adults possess this skill in excess of the rank and file of adults? Present theories about the possession of extrasensory perceptions may clarify the general observation of this fine-order communication which children appear to lose as they mature and which is manifest among so-called primitive peoples. Our observations with this child and others concerning what we are likely to label "sympathetic understanding" have less of understanding than we have thought and more of feeling. What we call "sympathetic" is also more nearly empathy. It may be that this skill will be found to lie more deeply structured than cortical or subcortical areas.

When inarticulate crying gives way before learned speech, new skills, and high-order nuances of communication become evident, and fresh problems arise which demand our consideration.

Those communications seem most potent which carry affective values as well as concrete ones. Poetic expressions, proverbs, and religious concepts succinctly caught into words may carry pervasive qualities which we label positively with a most accurate word "impressive" and which negatively we refer to as a technique for rabble-rousing. Stuart Chase, Harry Overstreet, Eric Fromm, and others made us aware of "powerful words." Workers with brain-damaged children who perseverate have found it worth while to build a working vocabulary in which affect-laden words, even such unanalyzable syllables as the *st* in stop, are more serviceable to a child in helping him inhibit than less loaded words like quit, please don't, etc.

The ancient wisdom which attributed such power to specific words seems less esoteric. Pythagoras is said to have believed that a word correctly spoken, could stop the bear in mid-onslaught or drop the eagle from the skies. Some such weight is attached to words in benediction, marriage and funeral ceremonial, and the like. Hopes and fears, visions and dreams must lie fallow in the individual who conceived them except as he is able to clothe their nakedness with words. And these words must be of such a character that they not only speak oneself to another, but of such a nature that they also can be heard by the listener, who must fill those words with whatever meaning his yesterdays have provided him so that his experience gives back the echoing truth.

For the teacher, or the one who stands in a teacher relation to the less able, communication is of primary importance. It is our stock in trade, our tool kit, the badge of our profession. As we have come to see how little the learner can learn by being told, we tend to trust more the commonality of experience as before-the-fact necessity for communication.

The authors have repeatedly demonstrated in a graduate seminar that its members, faced with the necessity to learn a simple string trick, are readied by the frustrations, failures, emotional disturbances, and ultimate success they experience so that they can understand the problems of their learners better. Insight, easily communicable to others of like experience, finds language for itself from the commonality of experience, as can no lecture however inspired. In our work at Rayswift it early became evident that communication took on a fresh importance as it became clearer that what we had to say to children was much less a matter of transportation of items of fact from nurturer to nurtured, and much more a way of helping the child to greater confidence in himself as learner and doer so that he created his own knowing. This point of view adds to the complications of the nurture job.

The image of self that an individual holds at any instant is made up not only of what his successes and failures have taught him to regard as a definition of himself. It derives also from what he sees as he observes those about him reacting to his successes and failures. Other human beings in his immediate environment are always serving as mirrors reflecting back to him images of his competence and worth as a person. If this mirror-like service of his human environment gives him back an image of incompetence it is hard for him to see himself as succeeding. An able person can see his inabilities more plainly than his abilities if his human mirrors tell him he is one who "can't." An unable person frequently exceeds what appears to be his capacity because another's faith in him has stretched him beyond what he had recognized as himself.

If a child believes himself unable to succeed, some wise adult or chance circumstance can help such a one into an experience with success. He sang successfully in a school program. She played a part in the school play, and was acclaimed. Presently this aroma of success permeated the total self-image. He began to succeed in chemistry. She progressed in geometry.

Capacity appears to improve with successes in unrelated areas. This whole effect is greatly increased as it becomes verbalized by others and reinforces the doer's judgment of himself as he is continuously assured and reassured by the approver's words. The releasing and encouraging words are all real values and tools for nurture. With the schizoid, the discouraged, and the unable, the healing word becomes almost a requirement for survival. With the best and sturdiest of us it is likely that we misstate when we say, "I like that person." We may, indeed, but it is more than likely that it came to be true because that person has first helped us to like ourselves better, and therefore we are drawn to like him. "To love one's neighbor as one's self" may have other than the usual connotation. We may not be loving him any more than we do ourselves and that may not be love enough to make our world go either around or on!

2.

In spite of overwhelming evidence of the oneness of personality and organism, when one comes to the point of a reasoned decision he is likely to speak of that decision as though it were arrived at in a dialogue. "I said to myself," one says and does indeed have a concept of two points of view, two types of evidence being weighed. Our present purpose is not to undertake an explanation of this duality which is more apparent than real. We are, however, concerned with the assumption that there exists or is brought into existence an image of the self which is crucial to the triggering of the whole energy-expenditure program as each individual acts or behaves.

The term behavior is interesting. It comes from the verb "to have," with the suffix "be" usually employed to extend and intensify the action indicated in the verb. Also it appears as a reflexive. "Behave yourself," as though below consciousness it were recognized that no one else can behave him. If something frightens him, he behaves himself in whatever pattern of frightened action he feels is appropriate. He may run if he sees himself as a better runner than fighter. He may stand and fight if he sees himself as the conqueror. Or like Shakespeare's Launcelot Gabo, "his feet may bid him run while his head bids him stay," and like so many more modern of us, he stays, with nerve and muscle throbbing to run. To some of us it appears that this yes-no behavior increases as the conditions of existence change. We could run from the great beast of the forest, but not from the small one lurking in the testtube. To fight—if we are courageous enough to fight—requires different armament. The automatic, built-in "flight or fight" are nearly as obsolete as poison arrows, since there is no one to hit and no place to run from an enemy that does not pursue. When we face such ambivalence we are at least temporarily neurotic.

Dr. Horney[1] discusses three selves: the ideal, the present, and the real self, with the same implications as we find in the different images of self. The ideal appears to be substanceless, projected like a wraith before one, in which one's aspirations and wishes are given the semblance of a form. Such a self may be a useful tool in defining goals. It is damaging when the projecting self mistakes, through wishful thinking, the sign for the thing signified. Then he believes himself already grown to the stature he aspires to and ceases to make efforts other than those

[1] Karen Horney, *Our Inner Conflicts* (New York: W. W. Norton, 1945).

that will support his own delusion. In the mentally ill this may be a constant state. To most others it appears to take over now and again when the self protects the self against the pain and effort incident to actual growth.

Nancy was too long fed puréed vegetables. She resents having to chew the actual beans and peas. We hear this child describing her plate as empty of beans—a nice little girl has eaten every last bean—although every bean of the three served lies intact before her on her plate. It is taking this imaginative child a long time to learn that even if faith does remove mountains. talk is powerless over beans.

The present self might be construed as the self which is visible at the specific instant in which the judgment clicks like a candid camera, preserving one instant's movement as though it were a static structure. The present self may be a useful tool in the service of growth. It may be a negation of potential and hinder growth.

The "real self," a term never clearly defined by Dr. Horney, is in essence, it would appear, the essential basic organization of process which crowds up into action whenever crucial decisions and behaviors are indicated. The ancient religionist thinks of this self under the label "Lord of one's Being." He would impute to it a quality of inviolateness and abidingness which is characteristic of the process of growth and inherent in whatever that process structures.

We prefer to employ the term "image of self" rather than splitting the self into parts or considering each as a facet of the whole. By image of the self we mean that total evaluation which the self gives the self in the face of whatever demand life momentarily makes. This apparent fluctuation in the concept is not well stated with the term "image," for image can connote a fixed and finished static form. We wish the word image to carry the connotation of reflection. He sees himself as able to cope with life or as overwhelmed by it. The automatic processes which have become reflexive in species or habitual in the specimen respond in accord with the image the self holds. With circumstance as a mirror, the self faced with that circumstance sees a reflection of itself coping with the circumstance.

Since circumstance is a moving stream and the self is in constant flux, we have the possibility of seeing ourselves differently at every instant, according as the change within the self is marked and the reflecting media are active. Some circumstances can yield us such reflections as release ourselves to ourselves until it would appear that a potential, usually conceived as fixed in quantity and quality, increases. Great moments, we usually call them; but it is more likely that it is we who, catching a glimpse of our potential, are inclined to live up to that potential. It is we who are great in those moments.

Dr. Alfred Adler said that one must study a child as one comprehended a movie into which he had come too late for the beginning. One had not seen what went before, but must guess it from what was at the moment in progress, and what later came to pass. There is no such thing as arriving in time for the child's beginning since, as we have seen, he is already the recipient of the ongoingness of his species through aeons.

Heidi was not quite five. Her parents brought her, telling us of her present state and what they knew of the origins of her problems. It would be necessary, they said, to feed her since she could not feed herself. It was necessary for an adult to go to bed with her since she was otherwise unable to sleep. She could not be left alone in a room for a moment. Closed doors set her in panic. Also she would not be able to go up and down stairs without holding an adult's hand. She could not dress herself.

All this was explained by the parents as due to the fact that she had been born in a DP camp in eastern Europe, shortly after an older sister had died of starvation in a ghetto. The parents suffered from malnutrition at her conception and the mother was inadequately fed during pregnancy. Heidi suffered from a glaucoma eye, a disfiguring birthmark on the right side of the face, and a minor calcifying process in the brain. She spoke only a few English words and suffered some frustration in acquiring a new language.

At Rayswift she was with those who understood her native tongue and as has been elsewhere noted she achieved a language proficiency rather quickly. All these inabilities—can't this and can't that—were reflected not alone in the speech but also in the child's total being. Could she have analyzed and structured her image of herself for us, she would likely have said: "I am one who can't eat or sleep or dress myself without people helping me. I cannot go down steps or cross a driveway. Needing people as badly as I do, I cannot have a door closed between me and those who wait on me." It was easy to write a prescription. It was difficult to fill it. Manifestly the cannots would have to be exchanged for cans. If these operations were done too brusquely, we would set up further panic. Words alone could not be expected to set up a new image except as we were able to involve her in situations where her own experience would force conviction upon her. Where to begin?

It was possible that the closed-door symbol was deeper than our interpretation of shutting off the sight of adults. We would not start there. Possibly also Heidi's vision was imperfect and though her glasses seemed corrective, looking down steps with no tangible support might panic her. Going to sleep, often a euphemism for death, must be a scary experience to one organized around fear rather than courage. Not that for a starter.

That left only eating. Hunger would be on our side and on hers. So she was seated with other children her age at a small table. She did not eat. She drank her orange juice but ate no solid food. Supper time came. Milk replaced the orange juice. Again she drank but did not eat anything. It was easy to reconstruct the circumstances. With such experiences as those of the parents it was understandable that they should overemphasize food and that she should use "not eating" as a club over adult heads. A little more milk was accepted before bedtime, but the next morning she took up her fork and went to work on eggs and bacon, toast and jam. One can't had been replaced with a can.

Sleeping, that first night, was an ordeal also. The usual soothing things were done. The child was reassured as to where her parents were sleeping at home and where her adults here were sleeping. When it became evident that no adult was going to lie down with her, she began talking in a mounting hysteria about the door being closed. She was invited to get up and fix the door exactly as she wanted it. She pushed it back to the wall. And another half-way can took the place of a can't.

After a few days of experimenting with the approval brought by these new powers, we began gradually the conquest of the alone-in-the-room complex. There was no clue to the origin of this fear. It may have been a useful tool, which she had found by chance, for claiming adult consideration. It may have been nothing more than the bare fact of visible aloneness from which no human is completely free.

The room from which one left the house to go to the mailbox, a hundred yards away had windows which commanded the entire path. This seemed a good location for beginning to conquer the alone-in-a-room problem. The child was placed at the window. The attending adult explained that she would now leave Heidi while she went to get the mail, where possibly there would be something for Heidi. The child was bidden to watch how long it took the adult to go. The first time there was near hysteria. The next few times brought only tears, and at length these also passed. She had removed one more from the collection of her can'ts.

Going down porch stairs was handled by a similar pattern. First adults with and then without holding her hand, then big children with and without, finally peers, and then one day none of these was available and it was suggested to her that the dog, standing by, would take her. This was satisfactory for a time or two. Then Heidi graduated from the dog also.

Endless small aspects of living were one by one added to her powers, and we could begin to see her building a new image of herself from her own experience and re-enforced by the reflections sent back to her in the approval of her adults. By summer, six months after her arrival, she was able to be left with other children at the recreation center for a couple of hours. Circumstance, in the shape of an epidemic of mumps, which did not affect her since she had already had them, brought the necessity to go by herself or miss enjoying the particular apparatus she played with at the center. She decided in favor of the adventure and did not even hesitate as she left the car, calling her goodby back over her shoulder.

We were eager for her to swim, but she would have none of it. A young attendant wanted permission to try a trick. She bought a beautiful new bathing suit which in her near-adult wisdom she felt would be a motivation; but she had, as we adults usually do, reckoned without the child. Heidi knew a good deal about clothes. One thing she knew certainly; on no account did one get new clothes wet, so the inhibiting new suit was a successful deterrent. No progress was made all summer so far as the water was concerned. Other less trying items kept swelling our data, but we did not know that Heidi was also making her own cumulative record.

Many new experiences in independence were made at kindergarten where her achievement was about average. In the fall of 1952 the ice came early and overnight. It was clear and smooth. The older children glided skillfully in and around each other. The small ones were running and sliding on their boot soles. We never dreamed that she would try this. Our adult knowledge that the ice was last summer's fearsome water was not a hindrance to Heidi. To our surprise she ran and slid and came to a stop, still right side up. She turned and called to me, "Oh Miss Rasey, I got so many things I can!"

Whether the verbalization and/or the generalizing which precedes it has any special part in verifying the growing image of the self, we do not know. The number of times that a child has taken hold of life immediately after such verbalizations leads us to guess that there is something salutary in "naming the name" on the self-perception level, as there is when a child names new objects in his physical experience. It may also be that the observer sees better having heard the child name his experience. All observers have a bent to see that for which they look.

This experience in watching Heidi become herself increasingly, and that in the face of certain known handicaps and some suspected ones, has led us to assume for each individual the existence of an ever-present, ever-changing image of himself. We assume also that there is a common core to these images which must be on the "can" side if the child is to grow in his skill in humanity's dual role—tool and tool's user—in the transaction involved in doing. Subsequently he may see this image of himself amplified as an artistic doer, an accurate doer, a willing doer. But before these refinements can begin, it is first essential that the individual see himself as a genuine doer—as one who can. So long as he sees himself as one who cannot, he is lamed and blind to his own enhancement. He cannot try. This we believe is the right word. When it is said: "Well, the least he could do is try!" the actual state of affairs may be that "the *most* he could do is try."

We have undertaken to discuss this assumption in a general application. As an individual sees himself repeatedly as unsuccessful, he tends to take that negation as his characteristic image. It may even become a fixed image which gives but slowly to the most skilled therapy. We tend to speak of him as fearful, aggressive, belligerent. The label is never exact. It merely means he is often belligerent, aggressive, or fearful. A personality resembles a chemical in this respect. Most molecules are of the type that is characteristic of the substance, but the chemist does not expect that every single molecule is the same.

Labels are thus misleading. When we say a child is an aggressive type, or a belligerent type, or a retiring type, we are implying only that one of these is his most frequent pattern of response.

Individuals also hold images of self that vary from situation to situation. These changes may be determined by the internal climate. A preponderance of lactic acid in the muscles may make one see himself temporarily as a nondoer. Items in externality also condition the image.

Jim was a child in whom circumstance had developed inordinate caution. Even the placement of his feet as he walked gave evidence of concern that each was placed on solid ground. After two years most such cautious behavior had given place to patterns of assurance in action. One day the children were playing race horse. Each child played several roles interchangeably. He was a horse with his legs, a rider of his horse with arms and torso, and the announcer of the races with his head.

"Jim Brown, riding High Stepper in a jumping event."

Jim cantered around to the starting line, tapping his thigh with his improvised riding crop. He himself had laid a dining-room chair on its side to serve as the hurdle. He gave his signal as announcer and rode up to the chair but could not bring himself to jump over it. Three times this was repeated before he was able to achieve the jump.

We had been working with Jim as if this fearful pattern had

been overcome, as indeed, it appeared to be. We did not understand our lack of success until we observed this evidence that certain circumstances could still call forth a hesitant response. It is this changefulness which constitutes a major hazard to any nurture. Here perhaps lies the area in which the nurturer as an artist rather than as an artisan is most clearly seen. The teacher whose high sensitivity to the state-of-being of the learner detects insecurity in the image, sees the learner's inability to release energy to action. Under this circumstance he does not over-urge the learner. When he does the result is too often failure; and failure is infectious.

He can wait if he has to and most often the learner has to be waited for. Whatever he wants for the learner, or the learner wants for himself, or whatever our society believes it has a stake in, will go forward only when the child sees himself with a fighting chance to succeed at it. No one goes to his own known defeat as if he were running to a fire. The whole nurture process becomes wasteful except as the learner believes he can learn.

Perception of externality serves primarily as a stimulus to action in our relations to external items. Perception of one's self serves as a trigger to action. If the image one has of himself is reflected in his state of being and these two items combine to release or withhold the energy essential to the action, it will be necessary to rethink much of our present educational procedure. We would need to implement positive image building which would mean more approval and commendation and less condemning. There would be a slump in the market for red and blue pencils. There would be more evaluating and less correcting in the early stages. Once the pupil has a sufficient experience of success to be confident and success-organized, it will be time enough to help him to an interest in a greater perfection or exactitude. He will welcome being right and be appreciative of assistance to be right because he himself is intolerant of error rather than because his teacher is. He is then in possession of an attitude and a practice which makes for self-motivated scholarship. So long as he is correcting the mistakes to which only the teacher objects, he is a time-server. When he becomes concerned with correcting himself, we shall dare to hope for speakers and writers who respect their mother tongue and enjoy its accurate use instead of those, of whom we now have many, who are in awe of their own language and are afraid to speak it or write it. We might also expect to develop more thinkers and fewer collectors of right answers.

Finally we have had to revise our thinking about the role of the teacher or nurturer. The learner does the learning. Teachers do not teach him. He is his own teacher. The stuff upon which he learns is his own externality of things and people. Of these two, humans appear to be more crucial than things. The most crucial thing about the persons who constitute his human environment appears to be what they understand, know, and know about. What a child finds important in his circumstance is likely to depend upon what values are set upon the event by his nurturers. For one child a rainy day becomes a major calamity which alters the pattern of his doing and sets the color of his moods. For another child a rainy day is a condition for which he dresses differently and no more. Children see their world as through a glass, darkly or brightly, as their adults reflect or transmit it to them.

The learner can come to his nurturers, but the transaction is achieved only when the nurturer can open himself to the learner and the learner can open to him. In order to interpenetrate it is necessary that the nurturer understand the world closest to him, which is himself. His knowing, in whatever degree, will function for his learners only as he is able to demonstrate that knowing. Whether he wants the responsibility or not, the fact remains that our own choices and preferences are themselves contagious, and ways of life of young humans always have a considerable admixture of the choices and preferences of those in their human environment. The teacher's role appears to be one of *being*. To this, feeling and knowing contribute to that which results in doing. We are, then, what we do.

CHAPTER III

We Apply Revised Methods of Observation and Nurture

The man who discovers a new scientific truth has previously had to smash to atoms almost everything he had learned, and arrives at the new truth with hands bloodstained from the slaughter of a thousand platitudes.

—ORTEGA Y GASSET

1.

It is relatively easy to sit at one's typewriter and indicate theoretical order in complex concepts. It is another task in the midstream of every moment of the active life of a child to clothe those theories with words and deeds.

Living children in altercation over a toy, children learning the irking necessity of routine washing and combing, children gobbling their favorite foods and loitering over less exciting foods, make demands upon one's philosophy. They require it to turn into action. As any twenty-four-hour nurturer knows, a necessity to reach higher and dig deeper than one's conscious knowledge goes into answering these needs.

It is hard to meet situations as they arise in terms of a new knowing. Something happens that has to be dealt with. Recognition of this difficulty and the belief that others beside ourselves suffer from it has made us decide to describe the new directions we took as we found new points of view resulting from changes in assumptions. We have not come upon *the* answers but rather upon *an* answer, one example of what we have found to be a difficult task. To change one's mind is not so difficult, but to change one's ways to match the changed mind—that is difficult.

40

It is hard to describe the process of changing one's ways of acting. We found that the commonly assumed sequence of events —namely, thinking through a situation carefully, then acting— was often reversed. Although we did analyze situations in advance of action as well as we could, that was never adequate. We now accept the fact that we act and then examine the action to determine why it succeeded or failed. In short, a part of our new frame is to act and then theorize the action.

The teacher who sees how the development of the single child fits into total ongoingness of life has a measure for interpreting specific behaviors. When she feels something like eternity preceding this individual life, in the life of human kind, she views with more poise the misspelling, the greedy hiding of candy, the pajamas left to lie on the floor where they fell. With a history of triumph over cosmic obstacles these temporary ones assume a proportion in which one can work on improvement. In this state of mind, the nurturer is further relieved of tension as he sees time stretch ahead of this young human and after him.

The concept frees the nurturer from tension without minimizing the actual, vital importance of the present specific yet-to-be-learned-by-this-one. With a time of such projected magnitude stretching into the not-yet, the nurturer schools himself the better to the inevitable *waiting* which goes with growing. It is waiting for days as one waits for radishes from seeds, for months as one waits from hyacinth bulbs to hyacinth blooms. It is most akin to the waiting of years for the apples which must bud and flower before they can fruit.

A concomitant attitude, which derives from this one, can be useful in reducing the tensions of the nurturer—the realization that it is the grower who does the growing. It is truly life that gives the increase. The nurturer is never the giver. The nurturer thinks as well as he is able: in what total circumstance can this child best learn? When he has thought his best and taught his best, when he has so manipulated environment that it be as easy as possible to find constructive ways, the nurturer begins his vigil. He becomes the encouraging and friendly spectator while life gives and the organism enhances itself.

When the observer feels that there is a spot where his responsibility gives over to the larger forces in life moving in the evolution of principles and processes, the nurturer does not need to be consumed with self-pity, sorrowing that his best was not good enough. He need not be frustrated. He need only be alert to what life processes were denied by his assumptions or theories and with what powers and devices life's purposes were finally solved.

There was the episode of the gooseberries. For more than a year we had been at work on William trying to get some articulation between him and a job of work. He, like others, chose what task he would undertake to earn money. He would rake one half of the driveway, a stretch of fifty feet long and eight feet wide where twigs and bits of paper fell. This task came due on Saturday morning. It was no more than completed when he began to talk about the six days until it should be done again. He counted off the days, like the Little Indian song, every successive morning and night until his adults were beside themselves.

On July 4 I sat in the yard with several quarts of green gooseberries requiring "heading and tailing" for jam. William came by and inquired about my task.

"Gee, it takes long, doesn't it?"

"Yes, but boys and girls like gooseberry jam on their toast."

"But you don't eat it yourself."

"Not any more, but I like it."

"Is anyone going to help you?"

"Probably. They usually do. Especially with something that everyone likes."

"I like it. I'll help."

He was shown how to do it and given a double handful in a pan. This was my guess as to how long he would last on this boring task. He finished them and rose, brushing the debris from his clothes. I thanked him generously and said it would help greatly. To my surprise he sat down again and asked for more. For three hours he stayed by the job with frequent repetitions of finishing, rising, being thanked, and sitting again.

The self-chosen raking job even with his dawdling had never required more than fifteen minutes of work. Against this was three hours of sitting and doing a repetitive activity. It became a matter of discussion and he said: "I just saw you doing it, and I like to help. I didn't have to think about it beforehand. I can't not think it's coming and I can't do anything about it until the time comes."

We changed our ways. We skipped the driveway one week because it rained. We did no anticipating and discouraged his. At the moment the task was mentioned ten minutes before the doing, with "if you don't want to do it, you can do some other thing, but there is a three-cent bonus if the job is good enough so that no part has to be done over."

Four years later the child is able to bear the anticipation of a few days, first learned in anticipating some pleasant outcomes, and gradually worked back to the humdrums of indoor and outdoor housekeeping.

He is not an enthusiastic worker. Perhaps he will never be. But he does well what he does without griping. On his twelfth birthday when we were taking account of all his skills, this improvement was expressed: "You can remember when it used to be so hard for you to do the drive, and now you do it nicely without any fuss? That's fine and grown up. Why do you suppose you had that trouble?"

"Well, I think I was just born not liking to work, but I learned to like it a little because"—with a sigh—"it seems to be the only way to get what you want if it costs to get it. But I don't like to think it's got to be and it's got to be. I like to see it and do it quick."

We found it necessary to act differently about permissiveness than we had been taught. It is difficult enough to formulate a general principle that agrees with one's facts and is practicable in the hour-to-hour situation. Such principles as we found still required special application to different situations and with different people. Also, the principles we evolved serve as direction pointers rather than specifics.

Our thinking in this respect led us to the conclusion that life never offers one a chance to apply his skill in using freedom without implying an area in which to use it. Authority, human if necessary, but preferably the authority of circumstance defines the field by fencing around it. We do not set a newly walking

child down in the midst of a trackless plain, on the theory that
he is going to do a lot of walking in his life and might as well
have scope in the beginning. We watch over his first steps within
the nursery walls. He graduates to the "run of the house," the
well-fenced locked-gate backyard. He "comes in" to new facilities
for practicing his skill in using freedom as his skill increases.
Some learn to use freedom over the earth crust and in the air
above it. Others must have the highways on which they drive
their cars fenced with speed signs, patrolling police cars, fines,
and sentences. We simplify our thinking about learning the use
of freedom by recognizing that strictly speaking it is not a right
to be claimed or a gift to be bestowed. Rather it is a skill to be
learned by practice, first within narrow and safe enclosure, later
by moving the authoritative fences farther and farther away.

What is describable in processes of nurture so conceived is
largely a way of connecting the child with his experience. "Hang
up your coat" slips smoothly off anyone's tongue, and slides with
equal ease off the child's consciouness. He may not even hear it.
He, his coat, and his value-judgment are involved in: "Wouldn't
it be better to hang up your coat?" "It seems to me it would be
better if you hung up your coat" gives an authoritative fence
around a permissive situation. It offers the learner some help,
just as holding onto a hand may help a child learner to walk.

When the child's attentiveness is challenged by a question, he
experiences freedom in choice with the customary payment for
the choice one makes. This is the prerogative of the free. It is a
drill exercise in the use of the skill of free acting. The most automatic obedience to the command of another can yield only a
greater skill in obedience, the skill most valued in a slave and
useful to a free man only after the power of the law has been
derived from the consent of the governed!

Two children had been playing with an express wagon. They
had left it in front of the door. "Whoever has been playing with
the wagon had better put it away, don't you think?" asked an
adult who was passing by.

"You got it out," one said.

"You played with it," countered the other.

"You."

"You."

"Both of us better put it away. She doesn't mean maybe!"

The concept of ongoingness gives time for growth; it has its sights set on the future. Channel marks are preplaced for marking, but progress from one to the next on a winding stream is predicated on the whereabouts of lights ahead. Children, like adults, live in anticipation. This forward sighting is done by long-range purposes. Pine cones watched all summer for potential Christmas tree decorations yield the learner more than going in search of fallen cones to meet a freshly risen necessity for them.

Summer-painted sleds with burrs freshly tightened on-goes into tomorrows. Seeds that will be flowers, bulbs that "will tulip" as one child stated it, small plants that will "turn into tomatoes" as another says—these are all acclimatization of the specimen in his ongoingness with species.

"You know how come this carrot is a friend of mine and tastes so good?" inquired the young philosopher. "It's because I knew him when he was just a yellow picture on a seed package and one seed in a row."

Try to duplicate that experience for Jimmie at two bunches for a quarter at the corner market.

The same child and I prepared the pansy bed. Tomorrow the plants would come into bloom. We dug the soil well and foreknew our bed. Should dark ones go at the back, or should we put the yellow ones there? Finally he settled back on his five-year-old heels and said: "My, but this is going to be a lovely pansy bed." I agreed. A moment's silence and he said: "You know a pansy bed that is going to be is almost as pretty as a pansy bed that is."

These quaint phrases may be smiled at and passed over as childhood's unspoiled views. They may also be seen as a readying process for larger goals and wider visions. The only distinction between this child's way of seeing in this case and in the research which has become his life's ambition lies in the material upon which it is exercised.

"I've found out," Jim announced one day, "that all the lady horses are riding horses and all the work horses are boy horses." He was five and greatly interested in boy and girlness beyond the human level. "That's queer," an adult responded, "when I was like you, the horses I knew were the other way about."

"Well," said the young researcher, "I guess I just don't know all the horses in the world yet."

Perhaps this whole ongoingness is a question of recognizing one's place in it and expecting greatly of the future.

2.

The assumption that the organism, a child, is before all else a quantum of energy required changes in our effort to conform to it. Following the assumptions of biology, we accepted the concept that the organism itself is the result of the first law of energy in operation. The organism is the structure that the ongoing, given, and inevitable process has built. He does not so much *have* a body as he is one. What else he is are further emergent structures built by the energies he is, in and by means of their process. While this continuous interacting process and structure goes on, a second law is operative—the energy is spending itself out from center until all is spent. In the nonorganic areas the spending appears to go on directly until entropy has established a rest or equilibrium from spending. In the living organism and particularly in the complicated human organism the exchange of one type of energy for another tends to slow the dissipation in what Schrödinger has called a "negative entropy."

The acceptance of the energy assumption has as its corollary the fact that energy transmutation is the way of life, serving various growth processes in turn. Here with negative entropy, as with entropy, the process is a function of time, or time is a function of the process.

At any rate it takes time. We discovered that, to make good on this assumption, we would need to increase greatly our watchfulness of how the whole creature spends itself. From the action patterns we can observe we must make inferences as to the values which determine the organism's or person's choices. We must try to see what energy he has available for spending. We must evaluate the success he has with this expenditure of energy. When the organism is ineffective with its spending, there are several places to look more deeply in the interest of his nurture. He would like the fruit from the branch above his head, but he lacks the knowledge of how to grapple the branch with a garden rake and draw it to him. Ineffectiveness may be caused by lack of know-how in the action patterns in relation to the goal. It may be also without purpose. No desires are strong enough to constellate any action patterns; or no desire is sufficient to release the all-important endocrine substance required to release the fueling sugar. Finally, there may be no fuel. He may have no experience of the cherries and no value-judgment toward securing them. He may be too undernourished and so under-fueled that he cannot make the effort. Obviously each lack requires different treatment.

If these items are viewed separately, one might try to teach how to use the rake when the small arms had not the power to raise it off the ground. Or we might give a taste of the fruit to encourage more goal-directed, that is purposive, action. He now knows how good it is but may still be too low in energy to try to fuel the purpose. We see this plainly in the starving child "too weak to lift the cup whose contents might renew him." It is more difficult to detect in the less tangible commodities and in the areas in which the signs of starvation are not to be seen in sunken eyes and atrophied muscles.

Yet scarring cruelties are perpetrated by well-intending but undiscerning nurturers, when an undernourished, underclothed, underloved child fails to wax enthusiastic over a project designed and able to release normal children into activity.

When a new child arrives at Rayswift, he meets the other children. They have usually been told that he is coming. "Who would like to show him around?" and quickly thereafter, "Which one would you like to have as your guide?" Choices, often surprising to the watcher, are made.

James—diagnosed as a childhood schizophrenic by a reputable psychiatrist—chose and was chosen by Heidi. She was his junior by three years as birthdays count it. And this occurred in spite of the fact that part of his difficulty was attributed to sharp conflict at home with a sister a year younger even than Heidi. There were three boys present of his approximate age. Did he recognize the child as a stand-in for his sister? Was he more accustomed to girls? The real motivation proved to be that he hardly knew her girlness from boyness. He was aware of his superior height and strength which he demonstrated again and again. After weeks of close association with her, he began to outgrow her and to gain confidence. After two marked school successes—telling the whole room the Peter Pan story and playing the part of a string of tinsel on a Christmas tree to his own and his classmates' satisfaction—he sought out the boys of his own age group in preference to the little girl. "I like Heidi, how she looks," he once said. Her blemishing birthmark was a beauty mark, or perhaps a badge of kinship with one similarly burdened, as he conceived himself to be.

After a few days' observation of the child's total spending of himself, we undertake to formulate a theory of what his way of life, his spending pattern, is. We do such formulation as a point of departure and not as a frame of reference. We do not say, "This is a schizophrenic. He will be withdrawn. He will be quiet. He will perhaps not be able to support cutaneous sensation of another's touch." What we do say is, let's watch him act. He could take her hand, but could not tolerate mine on his shoulder. He reached for my hand and removed it. He sat alone while the others clambered over the adult reading a story. "Want to come where you can see the pictures?" He bounded from the chair and then, not able to take the impact of eyes, turned his back until the reading was well in progress. Plenty of purposive behavior available. Plenty of energy to fuel it. What then?

A detailed story of Jimmie comes later. Here we may say only that Jimmie from his earliest months had given evidence of exceptional ability. His human environment from eighteen months to three years and the onset of his difficulty had been in the proportion of six adults to one baby: two doting grandparents, enjoying, perhaps exploiting their first grandchild, two parents with their first offspring, a bachelor uncle, and an unmarried aunt. Each took his turn at showing off the baby and teaching him new things, until the pressure of an adult was the signal for exploitation and fatigue, and turning in and away was a survival technique. A small child cannot hide far, and failure to save himself by these devices naturally led to explosive manic demonstrations, essentially those of rage.

Small Henry—with a two-year malnutrition from an inadequate though supposedly therapeutic diet—showed ineffectiveness in gogetting. No purpose was available. As growth began again on medication and protein diet, purpose aplenty was in evidence, and in a year's time his nurturers spoke of him as a stubborn or persistent little fellow, who knew what he wanted and often got it.

The theories we formulated for both these children began to be tested at every step: E. E. G's, blood counts, bone x-rays, Wechsler Grid interpretations of past growth history. The difference lies in the fact that no violence was done the totality while the part-processes and part-structures were being studied and their interrelationships were in evidence.

Finally, when all is viewed together, life is action and action is the visible product of energy released. As with less complex engines when the body doesn't deliver the power we anticipate, we undertake to examine its inner workings, its power potential, and its power delivery.

3.

When we begin to observe, we immediately discover that acting and behaving are ultimately a function of muscle. The fashion of naming the musculatures from their geographical location can be misleading. Taken in terms of function we would group the muscles in this way: (1) the muscles of the torso and legs act as agents of behavior in balance maintenance and locomotion; (2) the muscles of the torso and arms are functional in getting and fending; (3) the small muscles in the back of the neck, about the eyeball and certain pairs about the mouth, the fine adjusting muscles of the fingers and toes, in their various locations, furnish specific accommodation of muscles or nerves to the nuances of the great muscles' functioning; (4) the muscles around the eyes and around the mouth together comprise the expression of the face. The face might well be called the organ of social adaptation. Here we observe the only sets of muscles whose actions are labeled with the term *expression* although in all cases the behavior of the muscles is the expression of what has earlier been *impressed* by the individual's own experience or that of his forebears inherited in tissues themselves and probably inherent in them. (5) Finally, the tongue constitutes the fifth classification. It has many functions in other forms of life besides the human, but it is most highly specialized in man. It is the only muscle graduated to a new function. It is active in a most crucial fashion since it bridges the chasms between person and person by means of speech.

Much can be read in the behavior of these muscle systems concerning values that trigger and pattern muscular behaviors that are judged appropriate to serve these values. We believe that such patterns are clear indices of the state of being of an individual at any given instant.

We believe that the state of being at any instant determines the way and the extent to which the organism is able to spend itself at that instant. Secondly, we put more reliance in these muscular indices of what the total organism is going to do in the immediate future than in any other data derived from tests, measurement, records of past performances, and the like.

The organism acts as a whole, and therefore the whole contains in it the relative weight of all component values, however small and apparently inconsequential, which no analytically derived values could yield. We could not assess accurately what the millionth of a grain of thyroxin will contribute to the behavior if we examined it apart from the total process.

Finally, this total state of being that determines the organism's behavior at any given instant is a function of the image the organism holds of itself.

As we begin to look at a child we try to see how well he has adjusted to his balance problem. Does he lean into next steps and the future as one avid to get to a projected place? Does he lean into the future like one possessed to get anywhere which isn't here? Does he hold solidly and often stolidly to a balance, once established tensely maintained? How does he go? As to a triumph, or to disaster? Does his going anticipate his getting there with arms out? Does he hold back, tolerating what he did not know how to alter and allowing circumstance to break upon him? Does he drag his feet to make a brake on his going? Does he walk as though floating above the surface? Does he shuffle, too fearful or too despairing to risk losing an inch of contact with the earth crust that guarantees his balance? Why have we used the term shuffle to describe the gait of the old, the infirm, slaves, prisoners, vagrants, halfwitted? Why do we use the term elastic step for the young, the eager, the purposive, the well, the successful?

Are fingers lax and purposeless, eagerly questioning, idly wandering, grasping, grabbing? Do eyes search like fingers prolonged? Do ears prick up? Does the eye or the mouth expression open to receive life or tighten grimly to exclude it? Does his tongue run on to secure the safety attention brings, run on in an attempt to annihilate silence, more feared than sound? Does he build language bridges easily, slowly, well? Does he refuse all bridging, hiding in his silences or his stammering?

All these are broad brushes. They paint in broad strokes. The answers to these questions concern backgrounds and major figures. Their thousand nuances point and highlight or blur and shadow. Through these we come to see how the child *has* himself, and therefore how he *behaves* himself. Knowing his present state of being gives us specific guides for attempting relationships with him. Unless we know, action is blind, and when we are also blind, we cannot lead the blind.

Thus these assumptions concerning action lead us to look, but in looking to see. Much later and with much deeper insight we shall have to seek the causes of his behavior in the deeper knowings and feelings and doings of the child. The first question is what are his behaviors? With these once established we can then look for their origins, the better to help any child that requires changed behavior for his own fulfillment.

Finally we examine the effectiveness or ineffectiveness of his action. Did he get what he wanted? At this stage we are not primarily interested in any purposes but his. If he knows how to act effectively to get what he wants, he is teachable enough to learn objectives that we, while we are responsible, prefer for him. Now we want to know how much he "can." Later we will be concerned with the nature of his goals.

Observations after this fashion make clearer a theoretic knowing, namely, when action is ineffective, the organism tends to discontinue that line of action. When the action is effective, it tends to fix that pattern of behaving as axiomatic in similar situations. These principles are useful tools in education. The whole question of effectiveness, or the effect of one's action, leads directly into consideration of values, particularly those given the label of ethical, moral, spiritual, religious, social.

CHAPTER IV

We Analyze the Role of Purpose in Human Behavior

Our hypothesis sees in purpose, however, rather than in memory the process common to life and mind.

—Edmund W. Sinnott

1.

There is a difference between leading one's life and being led by it. Animals move from failing pastures and water holes toward fresh fields and springs, activated, it appears, by the needs of their tissues. Man, with his special talent for asking whether and why, possesses the potential for self-leading as much in advance of his nearest relatives as a cube exceeds a square. It moves him and his kind into another dimension.

We are unable to trace, or even to define accurately, the part-processes by which the organism passes from question to action. The action is all we can see. Its pre-processes must be inferred. He appears to ask: "Is the apple worth having?" If his judgment gives a yes answer, it appears to move directly into a declaration of intent to get it. Then the intent is implemented. He begins to climb the tree or search for a long stick as experience or ingenuity suggests. Next he carries out his plan and finally the achievement of the apple in his hand or the vision of it still fast to the tree furnishes him the fourth stage. All four of these stages have from their inception been feeding back into him such values as are usually lumped under the label "experience."

The new directions toward which our own questioning drove us in the observation of this complex in children indicated to us two things. First, *to purpose* is a learnable and teachable skill.

While maturity plays a large part in the scope and duration of a purpose, it was possible to increase both by nurture. The second new direction derived from the first, namely, that if purpose could be cultured, we should undertake that culture, and for that task we needed to know a great deal more than we did. We needed to learn about what we might call the anatomy of purpose. Is there a part-process in which values which might appear in random movement, like steel filings spilled on a sheet of paper, lie in random pattern until the introduction of a magnet puts a specific order upon each particle within the field?

Every teacher has seen both group and individual values leap into pattern and surge into action too fast to reveal the sequences involved. Thinking in these fields has led to the so-called field theories of psychology in which both terminology and concept have passed from one discipline to the other. We needed to know more than we did about the time element in these processes. It is an oversimplification to dispose of unfulfilled purposes as the result of a too short attention span. Is the length of time in which a purpose persists linked with the maturity of the purposer or with his value systems or both? Is the complexity of the purpose he can espouse and maintain related to either or both of these things?

We can now see that the process, while a continuous one, has a certain segmentation which we may set off parenthetically for study. While one child may be stopped from picking the asters by a three-foot embankment, another child can not only climb the embankment once but can also retrace his steps and return with clippers in order to achieve his purpose from which an obstacle has temporarily deterred him. Still another child has not sufficient freedom to entertain or to espouse a purpose he did not initiate himself. If carrying through a purpose were a task like climbing a flight of stairs, the first steps would have been taken when the child had decided he wished to go up and a second step when he released himself to climb. A third step is taken when the doer is able to support a continuing release of energy, to keep on climbing until he gets to the top. Once he is at the top looking down, the process has built a structure, namely an experience, about which he may or may not be evaluative. If he does weigh his experience and this most recent has-been joins the brew of all his yesterdays, a fourth process is invoked which also calls for rethinking since those who are said to "learn by experience" seem to learn well. If this process is also one that can be nurtured, we wish to know that fact and the processes by which it occurs.

Our observations lead us to practice as careful a discrimination between the above stages as we are able, for most practical reasons. To insist that a child complete a task because he began it, when he may not have been able to give more than a token acquiescence to it in the first place, is worse than folly. "I don't really want to make a sled. I'll bust it up for the fireplace," is a poor place to teach persistence. "Why should I say to the boys that I don't want to have anything to do with stealing the cherries, when I do?" inquired Nancy when an adult suggested a way to avoid complicity in a tabooed project.

We have learned to present purposes on the idea level first: "Would it be good idea to shovel a path to the ice?" brought the comment, "Yes, that's a good idea, but who wants to do all that shoveling?" There were no takers. Here the adult is free to say, "No path, no skating," and the path will appear, but so will protest against the labor involved and against the compulsion of the adult, a sense of helplessness that they as smaller people are pushed around by large ones. No one knows how far the poisoning contagion can go or with what degree of tenacity it can cling to plague a person into adulthood in his attitude toward work.

One often hears these practices criticized. "Life is not like that," they protest. "Good things are often the other side of arduous and boring labor. Such soft methods deprive the child of his experience in drudgery and effort." We would answer by saying that the first is a truth indeed. He must often spend himself to achieve his ends.

It is for this reason that we should like a child to have experience early and under nurture conditions in the two skills here involved. We would like him to learn to choose for himself what he will spend himself for, and second, we would like him to learn what he purchases with the spending of himself or fails to have by not spending. We should like him to learn early how his hours and his days resemble his coins, because once spent they are not available to spend again. Learners are then neither cloyed with effort unwillingly spent nor at the mercy of other people's evaluation.

He who has the skill to select his own purposes for spending himself is the only free man. No matter how much gain the work of an individual may provide for no matter how wide a group, it is slave labor if the labor is not self-selected. Here we see how inevitably democracy and the practice of equality constitute the only growing soil for freedom, and why freedom is the only skill from which the worth of the individual and the practice of democratic skills can evolve.

Charges often brought against the so-called new education are phrased in such fashion as: "So you want him to do just as he pleases? Whatever he wants he must have!" These criticisms must be met with the obvious fact that it is not what *we* want, it is a question of the way the organism operates. I personally would like to drive my car upstairs. I can't. It isn't built for that business. It is a fact of human construction, not a matter of educational philosophy, that the organism has to want to operate on some level before it can procure for the muscles the stored sugar with which to move them. "Want to" is a tricky phrase. Its proponents use it in a technical sense. Desires, "want to's," are functions of the subcortical areas closely related to endocrine flow and smooth muscle action. Its opponents appear to hear it in terms of whim, passing fancy, or as a temporary fighting device against those who want otherwise.

Many parents complain of willful children without appearing to notice that a single willful person cannot exist. It must always have a second willful person to will against! Punishment and reward, pain and pleasure, whips and fines can only command his wanting to avoid a present hindrance to his own purposes. Men have been tortured into confessions of crimes they did not commit. The place where each forsakes his own purpose is the place at which for him the price is too high. For some the price of death was less high than freedom. They did not confess.

Education for the good life is not only a question of the doing or not doing. It is a question of improving the order of man's desiring. When the quality of his desires has become sufficiently in tune with the actualities of his life and his social group, we will glory in his having what he wants, for what enhances him will do so only as it first enhances others. Again the emphasis in his education needs to fall on the wanting and not primarily on the getting. Before proceeding to a more careful examination of the progress in purpose with the children, let us look at it within an area with which most of us have common experience.

2.

Long ago, study in the area of purpose revealed the necessity to rethink our terminology. Our first conclusions were that there was a sharp difference in the way different people used the term "purpose." We tried to define the process in terms of its inception, its destination, and the path it took from one to the other, and all our analysis increased our confusion. Finally with our eyes upon people in process of carrying out their purposes, we came to another and simpler understanding.

Mr. Adams sits by his fire. His pipe is drawing well. His dog is drowsing happily by the fire. "Someday," the gentleman muses, "I am going to shut up shop, just turn the key in the door. I'm going to buy myself the best car I have ever owned and start on a tour of this country. One of these days . . ." The all-present author hears this comment. Some days later he encounters Adams, and says: "So you are going to retire, buy a new car, and tour the country?" "Yes sir, that's what I'm going to do, but don't hold your breath till you see me start. Talk, you know. Just talk. Likely die with my boots on, while on my way to the office."

We all know this stage of "thinking about what I'd like to do some day." We know someone whose purposes never bear more tangible fruit than talk; we know in our own flesh purposes of our own which appear to die aborning. In terms of our energy-purpose-effect sequence this is hardly purpose, or perhaps it is an arbitrary zero in purpose from whose near absence we may begin our measurement. If it were possible to see all that enters into such "just talk," we might be surprised at what it contains. As the burning glass may gather the parallel lines of light, bend them into a common intensified beam, focus it upon pith or paper and make burning come to pass, so it is likely that this which seems imperfect purposing is in fact its earliest stages from which it may or may not emerge firmly re-enforced, a strong energy pattern, moving over a defined path toward a specific objective.

Time and other potent forces are spent. One day Adams sits before his fire. This time his pipe is cold beside him. A table is drawn up beside him. It is covered with catalogues. Some advertise cars uniquely equipped for travel. Some have small maps on their backs and glowing descriptions of scene and facility for fishing, hunting, camping, and the like. Now what has become of this "just talk" purpose? It has come through some focusing process. Some day has become a defined *this day*. The choice of cars has narrowed from "a good car, better than I ever had before" to a particular make of car, with specifics of one and another kind which meet his more clearly defined purpose. A heavy line on the large folding map has become specific also. It has been selected from the great number of ways there are for circling or crisscrossing our country. One feels the pulse of a stronger power even though the same man sits in the same chair. A vast number of selections have been made in time, in space, and in circumstance. Yet the purpose is not yet overtly in process of fulfillment.

Early in our studies we believed that this stage was not a stage but another use of the term "purpose" put upon some action following some decision. Now we are thinking of it as a second, much more energized stage of purpose which has already passed from its inception in the idea, or ideal, stage. It has begun now to take on definition. It is still existent in the chaotic future, but it is now visualized specifically rather than generically. It has a place on the time line now, next week, this spring, a date as specific as is the projected car which even now sits in some showroom or moves on some assembly line. It has a hereness and a nowness which brings it inexorably nearer to the just-now than to the not-yet.

Now there comes a day when all these are actually focused. This is it. It is this. Outside at the curb stands the old car, faithful as ever. Its owner may look with something like guilt at its passive waiting for him to call it to life with the turning key. "In half an hour," he says, "I'll be driving the old crate over to the garage for the last time. I will be leaving the keys which have been part of me for the last two years. I'll give them over as the car goes in as part-payment on the new, the stranger car, which, near as it is, still exists in the not-yet so rapidly becoming the now."

The half hour is over. The key has been turned. The obedient engine roars into action. The car noses out into traffic, turns at the will of the driver and comes to a halt in the garage from which it will emerge next time as somebody else's possession. Our man will emerge with a new shiny, untried creature, or nearly a creature, in which or in whom, according to the fancy of the new owner, there is room for pride, hope for fulfillment of dreams long dreamed. In a matter of moments man and car unite. Its wheels and fenders, its pulsing power become extensions of the man himself. This purpose has been consummated. While we comment, "Well, that is that," new purposes have already begun to shape, and life begins to flow into new channels.

Here is purpose in process as we once called it. If our first stage was the idea, in the second stage the idea takes on definition. It becomes real. Then the third, more real than reality, is the stage of actuality. It is the "it has been done" as compared with the first "wonder if there could be," and the second "let there be." These we have decided do not differ in their natures. They are merely ever more intensive, ever more actuated stages of the earlier intangible, unlabeled, formless one.

Thus it was, by some such processes which can be described more quickly than they can be worked through, that we came to observing the purposes of children in a new way. We wished to understand much better than we did the part the purpose process plays in the total sequence from desire to effecting that desire. It could, we felt, point up the differences between those who never get a purpose past the talk stage and those who can define and lay out, but do not bring into fulfillment the goal envisioned. We wanted to know more about this for our intuitions led us to guess that those who failed to "do great deeds" and were vaguely content to "dream them all day long" might have alterable reasons for their ineffectiveness.

In other words, purposes as well as so-called mental and physical processes might possibly be nurtured. We turned our new instrument upon the affairs of children, but not without that lingering hope of the objectively-minded scientist, to find the spot of its beginning. Beginnings were too remote, we felt, ever to be known. They were part and parcel of primeval mud. Mr. Adams' wanderlust had doubtless been his by inheritance, laid down in the tissue of his forebears when the race of man was young and season and circumstances whetted his appetite for greener pastures, more accessible meat, and more plentiful water. It could not well be otherwise since some of the proto-plasm in this Adams was also in that Adam, if there were ever Adam, and if there were not, then still more anciently, in ditch water, and ambitious carbohydrate somewhere fermented by an earlier sun.

If we concern ourselves with a more exact meaning of begin-ning—that spot on time when some new thing was *inned*—so completely *in* that it was be(g)inned—then we are close enough to it to make some shrewd guesses about the conditions of its conception. Maybe Mr. Adam's favorite magazines wrote of far-away places with queer sounding names. Perhaps a colored movie of some unknown place or the memory which went back to a fourth-grade teacher's vivid concern with an area on the map. The specific is as varied as the individuals who react to it. They do, however, have certain common qualities. One is wonder—curiosity about those things not yet done in the flesh, but passively received from the accounts of others' doings until the desire to go and do likewise burns like a fire and consumes like flame all that appears as obstacle. The old paradox reappears: "By indirection we find direction out."

That method of indirection is confusing. When we want greater power in arms and shoulders, we feed the mouth. When we want greater deeds done for freedom, we feed the feelings. When we feel the need of loftier aspirations, we feed the spirit of man. Plainly, it is not enough that the body be fed its bread. Although a man does not live by bread alone, the bread is pre-supposed. It is more—but still not enough—that he be fed the wisdom of his forebears and be acquainted with their aspirations.

It is necessary that we stimulate and feed his wonder, that we help him to increase his own endurance span in pursuit of his wonder, until at least some one in every generation shall be able to say in the spirit of Job, "Though the truth slay me yet will I trust it."

William was standing by while his Christmas box was being undone. Serious disease and impairment made his own hands inadequate to the task. Small Nancy stood by with facile comment. "Oh, what a nice train," she said as there emerged from the package several small coaches, an engine, and a coal car, brightly painted and easily hooked together. One appraising look and she continued: "I could run that train better than he can. Let me take it. I can run it. I can let him play with it part of the time." The small hands which now closed over the small objects were completing the grab which had already begun earlier, when her perception of the objects and her relationship to them had grabbed as surely as did the hands now. "But surely," an incredulous voice is saying, "you didn't let her get away with that. Her facts are in reverse. It was the child who owned the train who should be letting her use it." Yes, that is true and it is also true that we did not at that instant reprove or educate concerning the ownership of the objects. Why we did it differently is a matter for later discussion. Let us interrupt the story to label what we have so far seen.

This circumstance like all others that any of us encounter is unique. It is one of the awkward aspects of life that they are all unique. Such commonality as they have lies in the interpretation the individual makes of it. It does not depend upon the facts themselves. Our salvation rests upon the fortunate fact that things and situations are not as various as the people who deal with them. "To be or not to be" has seemingly only those two solutions. Yet everybody has to deal with it and each finds varied ways of being or not being. Those who decide to be, by no matter what strange ways, have more in common among themselves than they do with those who decide not to be. Various people find a wide variety of ways to cease being, yet with more in common among themselves than with those who decide to continue to be. All the basis we have for grouping people into kinds and classes and types rests on this fact.

If we look first at the inception of that purpose, we see at once that there is within and between Nancy's sentences an assembly of aspects that are for her pertinent. "What a nice train" called for some reorientation. Her experience with trains which were bulkier and of the electric sort made it something of a surprise to see train, small train, no-electric train emerge. Between that sentence and the next, she had encountered the realization that this was not her box but William's. As an only child and grandchild, her six years carried little experience that anything coming out of a box could be related to anyone but herself. The eye-catching paint, perhaps the necessity to touch and who knows what, all funneled into that channel. All this contrived to give the child a sense of possession which was indeed spurious but which would also pass quickly, and then the child would be less cluttered with her desire to possess, and could the better receive some experience in ownership.

We will begin our observation by trying to see as far as we may back into those vaguenesses of preference and desire, value-judgments and fixed convictions. But most available and profitable will be those areas in which the third stage moves from readiness-to-do and passes by means of an act into doing. These are crucial areas for understanding, for it is with these doings that a person furnishes himself with experience upon which he can draw as new needs arise. Until his purposes have structured themselves by coming into being, he is without a past—without experience. His tomorrows are made largely of his yesterdays, which, when they were tomorrows still-to-be, had to pass through the narrow aperture of today wherein, fleeting and elusive as it is, all things come to be; and thus surely come, to pass.

Any beginning or end must be considered an arbitrary point established solely for the uses of our study. Actually no such halting places exist within the actual process. As cabbages are called ends when actually they are buds, and roses are called ends, though they are actually flowers, so the inception, definition, and actuating of purpose are three stages selected to aid our consideration only. They flow. They are not disparate.

Whatever the core of personality may ultimately prove to be and whatever its locus, we can be reasonably sure that it will be in flow, forming as individual function dictates.

Returning to Mr. Adams at the moment in which we cut into his reverie concerning his dream trip and the tools essential to it, we know that he is in a sense fluid in the hands of this thinking. As it washes about the solider facts of his existence, his thinking brings into conscious focus much that he cannot verbalize or otherwise communicate. Deeper in the core of the self lie equally if not more potent forces which remain below consciousness and operate from there. Tomorrow morning's obligations ride on free-flowing desires. He is "just thinking." At this juncture in the nucleating of a purpose neither he nor any onlooker can know surely whether this purpose will intensify itself and pass into another stage of ongoingness, or whether some constellation of values will take priority. He may decide to go on safari without a car, or dissolve the whole pattern and buy an annuity. To the individual in this stage of formulation there is no limit upon what he may pattern, yet so soon as one of the lines gains precedence over another and moves into tighter organization, then outer reality cramps the creator's style so that what he dares to dream of he does not dream of doing!

If we undertake to guess why this desire to travel is preponderant over other possible purposes, we shall be hindered by the lack of facts or a method for obtaining facts. The health and strength of his body is doubtless a factor. It is possible that superior strength and pulsing energy may make the desire to wrestle with actualities of nature effective in his unique picture. It is equally likely that a body of the type such as that recorded as belonging to Theodore Roosevelt may drive him to undertake proof that he is, more than the usual man, a master of circumstance and captain of his fate. Patrick[1] pointed out that those occupations which were full of uncertainty and hazard for early man are now those perpetuated as methods of relaxation: cooking outdoors, hunting, fishing, striding over a golf course, carrying a club and striking at small objects, camping to get the best

[1] George Thomas White Patrick, *Psychology of Relaxation* (Boston: Houghton Mifflin Company, 1916).

of circumstance in the heart of nature's wilderness, unmindful often that the boatload of equipment which is taken along somewhat alters the advantages which nature may have in the fight.

Feelings of inadequacy hold a high priority in the rejection process. Such a proposed camping trip far from civilization may quicken the pulse of one person and depress another, who may say: "That might be all right in the day time, but I don't like the woods at night." Or another may reject it as completely because of a fear of snakes, forest fires, etc. The fluid of self, unique from the yesterdays of the organism and of its forebears, carries the potential for accepting or rejecting at the point of its inception anything about which the self can dream. Within this fluidity one line of desire may easily neutralize another before externality has established boundaries. Yet the fact remains that readinesses, attitudes precipitated from earlier experience, feelings of all orders of intensity are crucial elements in the inception of purpose. Vision or dream, wonder or curiosity appear to be first stages for all things which come finally into actuality.

The sheer energy available to the organism may be a significant factor in the inception of purpose. The camping trip will make one set of eyes glow, and the owner of them may foresee: "A lot of portage for the boats, eh?" as though the anticipated strain were projected as fun. Another person answers the situation with an "All that work to play? You call that vacation?"

It is also possible in this early stage that an individual who is in sympathy with every objection and has no desire of his own to undertake such a project, nonetheless goes into it in terms of the value it may have for someone whose satisfactions mean more to him than his own first-order direct satisfactions. The valence which these and many other items may have will appear to be differently organized for the different persons.

Thus some aspects of this first stage, vague as are its components, are well within the range of education. It is possible that readiness for adventure can be taught. A preference for creating one's own facts rather than asking others questions can be taught. It involves the type of nurture provided. Subsequently we shall offer some observations upon what we have been able to do in this matter.

In what we have arbitrarily called the second area of purpose we can see that the process takes form. Selectivity pulls into a narrowing band the items which the organism chooses as axiomatic. The selecting process appears to be done as much by exclusion as by inclusion. It is a process of not this and not this but certainly this. In the case of the car-buyer, it is not this car, nor that car, but this other make which is the appropriate type. Not the week after this one but Tuesday of this week. The locus of the arrival begins to be determined, again partially by externals and partially by the desire of the individual. He selects from among several the method of payment of his car. He plots routes by excluding alternatives.

Now the organism becomes more active than in stage one. In that earlier stage he fed his purpose more as does the simple marine creature which appears to wait passively in midstream, letting life bear him what it has, and with a modicum of selection only accepts and rejects. In the second stage he goes out after his objectives. In the first stage he employed little beyond flowing reverie and impassive selection. In the second, he uses imagery to project the goals as if they already existed. He weighs and evaluates. He judges and rationalizes. He invests heavily of his experience. He shapes his proposed path of action. These varying types of mentation all lie in the areas of educability. He can learn to do any and all of these processes better and more expeditiously. At this stage there can be nurture of purpose and in terms of that nurture we dare expect an improved process and ultimately a higher order of effectiveness.

As the defined purpose emerging from stage two moves into stage three, the lines of energy have become enlarged as lines of purpose have fused. Adams had to discard his purpose to pay cash if he had to pay on contract. He had to select 160 horse power if 120 were too little to pull his trailer. Now he enters upon the final readiness. The hour to turn in the old car and accept possession of the new has been set. The time has come to enter the old car for the last time. The key is turned. A few minutes driving, a little delay with papers, and he and the new car move out. The purpose has been fulfilled. He has had one more experience with which to amplify his earlier experience.

This stage of a purpose appears more a reality than either of the others, for one can see him at it. His earlier feeling and thinking were not easily detected. His doing now is an open book. From that doing we must infer whatever we can about his earlier stages. Inference is our only tool there. This third stage is the one at which we must do our observing. There is no other visible one, yet we must protect ourselves from misreading this stage. It is no more important than either of the others. It is just more tangible, but like so many other tangible spots in human growth, it is too late to effect change. The process has already structured. It is in the earlier processes that change if any must be made. With this in mind we look differently and with different intentions at this third stage. Everything is here—the methods of doing, the evaluations which can make goal and process of arriving.

In the third area of the purpose process we see the lines converging into a single strand, somewhat as wires are bound into a single cable. The individual concomitants are singled out from the mass of possible ways in what appears to the doer the most appropriate patterns, and larger portions of his energy pass into the accomplishing of the task. Mr. Adams finally narrowed his purpose into the single "this one thing I do" sequence. He might have sent another member of his family to pick up the car or he might have had the salesman deliver it, but he rejected these, and singled out the sequence which ended in his driving off with a new car.

The components of this third area involve judgments, selections, and actions which are largely in the realm of the learnable. They are thought through in and by means of mental process which we understand how to culture. The action is carried out by educable striped muscle. It can be re-educated. It is here that the purpose is consummated. Its effectiveness can be guessed in earlier stages. Its effectiveness can be known only when the accomplished fact has become history.

This area is by the same token the least manipulatable of all the stages of the sequence. If Adams finds his digestion upset by his restrained emotions at the farewell to one car and the acceptance of another, and he has to draw up to the curb to await the restoration of his balance, or to have some other person drive, it presents difficulty. "He should have known better," we may say; but he didn't. He judged the not-yet badly. His purposes went awry. He was dependent on his fellowman to help him complete his purpose in a more spectacular if not a more vital way. It is at such spots in our encounters with the not-yet that many of our failures show; yet the failure proper may lie a long way back of where it became evident. The sad thing is that this episode in purpose cannot be altered here and now. It can be a point of learning, but the effectiveness of whatever is learned will have to await the next similar situation to become actual.

Alfred was nine, to offer another illustration, and due to a specific brain damage suffered occasional sharp aberrations in appetite, showing a need for sugar in great amounts. He had learned to watch the kitchen proceedings with great care and come in to get "dibbies" on the frosting bowl. He was so watchful that it was always he who staked the first claim. He was ungenerous with the less watchful children. On a particular day he had bidden for the bowl, with a girl at his heels but nonetheless behind him. "Alfred may have the bowl, but there may be some on the beaters, Carole, so both of you come back in a few minutes." When they arrived, the bowl was practically bare thanks to an effective rubber spatula. The beaters, less accessible to the gadget were well laden with frosting. Without comment he was given the empty bowl, and she the beaters. "I'm not mad at you," he announced as he saw that he had been worsted. "No, I shouldn't think you could be. You got just what you asked for," was the answer. "Next time, I'll just say: lick," was his comment.

"Why do you suppose," we inquired, "that it came out this way? Was it just because you said bowl instead of lick?" "I don't suppose so," was the slow answer. "I guess it is because I'm too greedy, always wanting it myself, instead of letting her have her chance." "That might well be. Being too cute trips us all up sometimes."

"Shall I give him one of the beaters?" inquired the other not so sugar-minded child. The answer was: "Suit yourself about that. I remember that he didn't divide with you last time. No one knows but he what he will do next time." "I'd be even with him if I didn't divide, but then he won't divide with me next time, because he'll have to get even for that. Here," and she extended a not-quite-licked beater. It would appear that her skill in human relations outran her skill in hygiene.

This occasion became good laboratory but how effective or ineffective it may be in modifying behavior we will have to wait to see until the next occasion when a similar problem presents itself. Perhaps most of our human behavior is of this type. After the fact, we see, but the fact is irretrievable. It is, however, re-education rather than education, and correspondingly expensive. This has been said before about experience. The simple prefix hardly shows how repetitive it is. The person must go back into his experience and take out—dismember as well as remember—what he finds pertinent to the new venture. It is here that the teacher functions.

3.

Our original, uncritical assumptions about environment led us to use such a term as "a good home environment" in our original set-up. As soon as children were introduced into our home environment, it became evident that our definition and imagery were inadequate. An environment dedicated to "Every Loveliness" had too much that was fragile and too much upholstery of delicate fabric to be lovely for the children for whom it was not re-dedicated. Even the furnishings became something different when viewed from the angle of facilities for growth.

Finally we came upon a proposition and a significant corollary which can be stated in one per cent of the time it took us to discover them. The proposition is based upon our discovery that feet on upholstery, muddy rubbers on the floor, a loose edge of wallpaper pulled into an unsightly destruction were not evidences of original sin in our children. They were evidence that children, who had no investment financial or otherwise in "things" in the house, had other investments and purposes with which temporarily their whole lives were involved; and these blotted out the memory of frequent admonitions to keep feet on the floor and rubbers on the porch. With the best intent in the world, these active, zestful youngsters simply could not be forever hindered by caution.

"What is a good environment?" we asked. We felt confident that a barren barracks-like housing was bad. Loveliness on some level was as essential as food for personality. Just cleanliness in antiseptic barrenness is depressing to most people. As usual, it seemed, the answer would not be found in any simple either-or situation.

It became a simple task to write the prescription but difficult to fill it. Environment must, we decided, be functional. Sturdy furniture with less fragile finish and upholstery would be the right start. It had to be some kind of lovely and have some kind of abidingness—a combination difficult to find.

We also learned that too plain and barren an environment afforded no facility for learning the care of "things." Our final judgment is that a physical home environment is serviceable to a growing child when it is made of furnishings, dishes, table equipment, etc., with a degree of loveliness or fragility he can care for without a preoccupation with care that will consume his energy beyond his powers to budget and still be able to pursue his own purposes.

The important corollary is concerned with the necessity to have a problem in order to have the facility for learning skill in its solution. Aluminum drinking utensils avoid breakage but give no facility for practicing care with glass. Unbreakable plastic dishes save wear and tear on nerves, but teach no skill in handling china. The same notions hold with the care of clothes, with eating habits at table. Too much training too fast can hinder more basic techniques for living.

The physical aspect of environment within doors is the easiest of the problems to solve. External environment is more complex. A yard to play in, a lake to swim in or skate on, and some rainy day equipment looked like answer enough in the beginning, but not for long.

"Let's go down to the highway," the new boy was saying.

"Miss Rasey won't let us play there," the regular responded.

I overheard the conversation and was alerted to it. One grows conscious of prohibition imputed to a person when one is concerned with training for self-direction.

"What do you mean, I won't let you?" I inquired. "I'll go down with you now if you want to go."

The party contained two seven-year-old boys, one carrying a fat little puppy, and a five-year-old clutching a bright new ball. Going down involved a downgrade walk of five hundred feet and a right turn to a narrow walk along highway No. 19. This is a state highway, carrying a large volume of rapidly moving traffic north and south. We stood on the walk a few moments watching trucks and cars dash by. The displaced air smote the small people like a blast.

"Hang on to puppy," called Jim who was unlucky enough to have some one else carrying Pudgy and unable to lay hands on his cat when the expedition started.

"What would you do," I inquired, "if Pudgy jumped down and ran into the street?"

Harry turned his wide open eyes at me and said: "Gosh, I'd just jump out to get him, I bet."

"You would? Then what would happen?"

"The puppy might get run over."

"And you?"

"I might get killed too. Gosh!"

"Do you know why this isn't a good place to play?"

"Well, sure. I might not run into the traffic even if Pudgy did. But Ralph might drop his new ball and he might not know better than to go."

"I do so," answered Ralph.

"Well, you see why I don't think it is fair for you to say I won't let you do something, as though I was keeping you from some fun you wanted to have, when it isn't that at all. It's just circumstance, like moving traffic, which really says that you'd better not."

The second's silence was hardly enough to let me feel I had got my point across. The next day, however, the same new boy said, "Let's go up to the far end of the lake and play explorer." And the same child responded,

"Unhuhh! We aren't—Circumstances, deep water don't let us play there until a grownup can go with us." Circumstances was a big word in a small mouth but it also carried a freedom-directed concept for at least one child.

Once more, however, we have to remind ourselves that a hazard-free environment would be hard to produce and would remove the facility for learning to handle oneself in the face of hazard. Trees of varying difficulty to climb, good swimming form in order to be trusted in the boat alone, denial of use of rakes and spades if left lying tines up or sharp edge exposed, do afford facility for learning caution but are not final with one lesson. This aspect of learning facility is often overlooked. The cost of instruction must not be too expensive. Anything in the skills area presupposes errors in learning. It is the task of the nurturer to provide learning facilities sufficiently hazardous to make the learning significant and not hazardous enough to make it terminal. The prescription we try to fill for our children involves the opportunity to learn by experience what wise doing is without involving unforeseen hazards of too high cost.

The important aspect of the environment is, of course, the humans and animals and other living things it contains. In any group of children all but the youngest one have the experience of children younger and less able than themselves who need their concern and help. All have experience of older ones who can help them and for whom they also can be helpful. The oldest child has the adults for this relationship; and youngest and oldest, the two most difficult places in a family constellation, have friends outside the family group.

We have found it wise that each child, even the least able, has labeled relations with someone of a cooperative nature. Older ones move toward adult responsibilities. Younger ones graduate from responsibility for sweeping a porch, carrying in milk bottles, feeding animals, etc. Tasks are often suggested but they are always self-assigned. Those for which someone would be hired are paid—50 per cent for the work, and 50 per cent for taking the whole responsibility for it. No responsibility, half pay. No work, no pay. This way, children soon learn what one remarked after having to be reminded and getting docked, "Well, I'm not going to take any more nonsense off myself!"

In fairness, however, it should also be told that another child who got fifteen cents instead of the thirty that would have been due had the leaf pile been carted off and the rake put away, juggled his dime and nickel back and forth, as he said feelingly:

"Gee, Miss Rasey, there must be some better way of getting money than working for it."

The adult human environment of these children, both trained and untrained workers, possess in common with most people an earnest desire to see children grow into fine people. All are selected and kept in terms of their interest in children. Six adults however do not always agree about means and methods for achieving the common purpose. We make such agreement among ourselves as we can and each is free to believe what he can. If one is overtalkative until the children go functionally deaf, this fact carries its own evidence when he has to call for help from another to get a response from a child. For the child this difference in values is not more confusing than it will always be as long as he lives with people. If he tries to live alone in a cave, he will have worse problems.

We try to assemble people who would rather laugh than cry when things go wrong. The realization of the long growth span helps to keep small things from appearing cosmic. Everyone tries to respect the affairs of children and to weigh their rights, but contrary to many thinkers we teach that there are such things as adults' rights, also. If a child is asked, "Would you like to take these things over to the big house?" and he says, "No, I wouldn't," he may be reminded, "But will you like to have me put down my magazine and pop corn for you when you ask? If you will some time want me to stop my play to do something for you, wouldn't it be good if you did the same?" We ask many questions of young thinkers, but we make few statements of our facts to them. When and if a child changes his behavior, the adult usually says, "Well, that's the way I thought it worked. Now you are being smart," or some like manner of referring the episode into the general and away from the personal.

Correspondence with environment is one of our oldest ways of describing the life process. We have mentioned here only briefly the modifications we were led into as we came to particularize what we had called good home environment. Perhaps the strokes are large enough to convey the theories we hold and the practices we evolved to meet our specific needs. Children select from all, as do we, the few to which they attend and which make the major features of their environments. They make their own laws, as do we, and as we do also, they then must abide by the laws they make. On the outer reaches even of the dark, the weather, the seasons, etc., if they say that the dark is a menace, menace it is, until such time as the child understands darkness as a state in which it pays to be cautious rather than afraid. These elemental areas lie remotely from the child, but as layer after layer is recognized as closer and closer, the same laws obtain. He makes his environment by what he attends and gives value to. Finally he comes upon his own internal environment—his "skin-limited" self—within which colloids and humors feed, cleanse and safeguard between the inner walls of mucosas and the outer ramparts of skin. His sea-water environing internal fluid he brought with him, as any modern traveler into new realms takes with him his essential oxygen and the wherewithal to maintain his narrow range of body temperature.

The tangible items in externality with which the organism is in constant transaction are easily understood. With man's tool of intellect, he is furnished with subsidiary gadgets to aid locomotion, maintenance, and the like. It is not so easy to assess or to provide the externality requisite for the maintenance and growth of those aspects of self which are implicit in that ancient knowing that man does not indeed "live by bread alone." We are primarily concerned in establishing what is personality's meat and drink and under what pressures or freedom from them his growth conditions are best maintained.

We are sure about his need for people, but we are not so sure what proportion of that human environment need be his peers, what part must be for his own nurture, and what part for him to nurture. Spiritual mathematics differs from that of common reason. To be the receiver, we are taught, is less good than to be the giver. What one gives is often all he has. What he has been at pains to conserve appears to be dissipated while what was divided appears to have been multiplied. It seems to us, therefore, that one needs to give and receive facilely in his human environment.

His need to be valued looms large, but to be overvalued is often to be pampered, and the pampered person is weaker by virtue of the pampering. This means that in this respect that human environment is most useful which draws the maximum amount of optimum effort from the child, with the adult ready to turn failure into success when the child's best is not good enough. The chief worth in status, or being valued by others, appears to be the help it gives the individual in coming to a more adequate or accurate self-evaluation.

4.

As skill in purpose increases, so does the image which the child builds of himself. The more success he encounters, the more he sees himself as one who is able. The more constructive his image, the more potent his state of being to release himself into life. We have had to change our direction in relation to self-image. As increasing maturity points his purposes and alters his values, his purposes and his pursuit of them bring him into ever closer relationships with people. His larger social function constructs his self-image with ever more valued social aspects. Only from people is he able to secure the elements necessary to construct an image of himself as social.

We had begun our work with children on the assumption that changed behavior would be able to follow only upon a changed conviction about one's ability to effect that change. We believed that these changes lay largely on the side of increasing the child's conviction that he "could." We had relied greatly upon the affirmations of his ability to do and generous approval of what had been done. In all of these we had been counting largely on the word which came to the child's ear from others. Potent as is the general trend toward an emphasis upon the positive, we began to doubt that this was enough.

In an earlier discussion of image building, Heidi was described as having a major problem concerning closed doors, complicated by fear of falling asleep or being cut off from supporting adults. Actually she was invited to get up and fix the door as she wanted it; but the meaning of that experience went much deeper.

A child who has been honestly dealt with by adults is better able to use adults' promises than those who have not. Heidi had this to her advantage. Parents had always kept their word. But we began to suspect that, as with any other area of learning, one avenue of access is not always enough. We already knew that a learner understood completely only what he could do. It is for these reasons that we do not argue with a fear. To begin with it is not amenable to reason. Its organ system functions when triggered by images of oneself as helpless, fearful, and alienated from one's self and one's kind. Feelings of inadequacy derive from experience with being inadequate. These feelings will be resolved only by experience with being adequate. Apparently this needs avenues of involvement other than the aural reception of another's word.

When Heidi began to be hysterical about the bedroom door being closed, and was invited to get up and fix it as she wanted it, her response required that she employ her whole self to rise and go to the door. As undisputed master of circumstance "door" or perhaps we should now say, "operation door," the whole self was engaged. She pushed it more violently than was required to open it against the wall. That surplus expenditure of self must have given satisfaction. Besides, the mounting hysteria which must ultimately explode is, at least after becoming visible, merely more energy than can be channeled. The act of getting up and walking, pushing and returning to bed drained off surpluses which must otherwise have taken internal avenues. We think also that a sense of confidence in one's power to control circumstance is experienced when one's own muscles put things in accord with one's own desires.

As we watched these areas both with Heidi and with what we saw in other children, we began to generalize this experience first into a philosophy and then into a method for implementing that philosophy.

We saw that a total organism response was not the sole means of developing the sense of "I can." Any part-process of behavior was a useful method. We saw, as we listened to the natural phantasy of children's play, that aspirations for the relatively near fulfillment of desired purposes were stated as matters of fact. "This is my pony, I'm riding the afternoon race" might well be understood in less ambitious terms; "my horse" was the convenient stick used by all and sundry in lieu of a horse. But it was actually a foreshowing of a purpose to ride a pony, never yet seen, which was to be delivered in the afternoon. "The after-noon race" was known to be a sedate walk around the drive as some one led the pony on which the erstwhile race rider sat in an ecstasy of fearful confidence or confident fearfulness according to his state.

We discover that the generalization before the fact can also be a useful mold into which to cast subsequent action.

"I'm too little" as well as "I don't know how" and "I can't" are obvious delayers of action when action is the main tool for the experience of "canness." It seems safe to suppose that one might expect such release when the pronouncement is positive. In terms of the image of self, generalizations must be thought of as the picture the individual sees inside himself and can show others only by means of words.

We believe and act on this assumption when it looks as though the child has had sufficient success experience to warrant a positive verbalization. When it does not come, we state or give some guide to its formulation, registering in our formulation and tone the surprise and satisfaction we believe will be his when he formulates.

We find such verbalizations more useful when they are indirect. Helen had a new bicycle for her birthday. After her first attempt on it she hid it in the shrubbery to stave off someone's suggestion that she learn to ride. Some weeks later, she got up from the table saying, "I'm going to ride my bicycle." No one commented nor did she wait for any comment. She was really talking to herself.

Fifteen minutes later we went out to see her, wobbling pre-cariously but still balanced and in line with gravity. Knowing how poorly she supported extra attention, no one addressed her directly. Instead one adult called to another. "Would you believe Helen has ridden her bicycle right around the drive? Is she good!" She made another round with less of the wobble, and then set the bicycle against the front steps while she announced to all, "I can. Am I good! I rode it around twice"; and being Helen, she stood and gazed at the bicycle for minutes, got on again, and went round, round, and round. By the time some hours later when she had her weekly telephone conversation with her parents, the success was well tied into her social fabric. "Will you ever believe it? Everybody thinks it's wonderful. I can ride." Evidently the parents questioned her about how far. "Oh, anywhere," was her answer, which was neither exaggeration nor fulfilled truth, for the space ridden over was just the round and round. We were happy to leave it at that, however, since we see it as projected purpose—the pattern ready for the molten metal to transfer its form from shadow to substance. We think it is of a piece with the reach that needs to exceed the grasp, the slack to avoid the terrific tensions which are part and parcel of the second-order purposing, when what one has "dared to dream of" has passed over into the higher order of what he has "dared to do."

We also discovered in working with Heidi's image of self that it was easy to mistake a specific problem for the thing it stands for in the child's hierarchy of values. We stumbled over Heidi's problem of lacing and tying her shoes. We looked for her difficulty in the threading and inept hands in the knot-tying job. We spent effort on teaching these things. Other more difficult matters she had already mastered. She put off attempting to try. She pulled one end longer than the other and seemed unable to correct it. Finally we came on the real issue. She had been sitting in a corner of the room with some toy. She was alone in the room. Both shoes were neatly tied. One of the workers came into the room, was called, and turned back to answer. When the worker turned back to Heidi, she had deftly untied both shoes and was kicking and sticking out her feet to be noticed. "Will you please tie my shoes?" she asked. Obviously these were no longer strings to tie shoes up. They had become strings to attach her to her adults by the tether of her needs. It was not the tying responsibility that was so hard to take. It was the helplessness which had to be surrendered, and you could almost hear her ask: "How shall I show how much I need them unless I keep them tied to my shoe strings?"

When such helplessness is employed with or without verbalization, it is an irritating regression to the nurturer. It should also serve as notice to that same nurturer how great is the child's need for the tangible signs that she is important to some one. It would be a "malfeasance in nurture" to force independence in shoestring tying when the real problem is unwillingness to surrender dependence on others.

At this juncture the nurturer's artistry has to come to the fore. She has to guess as accurately as she can at what point the learner stands. There is no prescribed right rejoinder. Any recognition of the wish to communicate is better than none. One person may say somewhat brusquely: "Here we don't tie strings for children who can tie for themselves." These are facts and will be arrived at in the nature of the case. The affect, largely negative in tone, could outweigh the slight positive affect that the doing brought. A preconceived notion of what one will say may betray the nurturer into saying what he has prepared to say. It is therefore probably better to stay empty-minded, the better to feel what is indicated as need. For better or worse, as the artist's creation must always be, the nurturer responded: "Yes, I guess that's right, but now you are here and, as you can see, all the others are trying for themselves. You are such a big girl now that you will want to tie for yourself and I see you are doing it very nicely."

When this type of labeling is used as reinforcement, the child may escape the need to save face by further refusal to act. She has the mirror set up for her in terms of her playmates, with the balance on the side of activity. She can go on trying for herself the rest of her life. She can, but there is no guarantee that if and when life grows more difficult, she may not regress to the need to prove to others that she needs their support. A few weeks later when exactly this happened, she reverted. This time she needed only to verbalize it.

When one *has himself* as possessed of many capabilities, the state of his being is "success organized." The individual is mounting from a can-doer to a doer.

Our practices which have resulted from our assumptions concerning the perception of the self, or the image of the self, have tended to intensify rather than change our former procedures. As has been pointed out by Schilder[2] and others, the most

[2] Paul Schilder, *The Image and Appearance of the Human Body* (London: Kegan, 1935).

intimate aspect of that perception, the body image, does not accrue to the individual out of his own perception of himself. Even his body image is derived and modified by the image he has of other bodies than his own. His image may amount almost to a reflection, seeing himself reflected in others. He may come to that image by comparison, by contrast, by fusion in physical contact with another.

We are here concerned primarily with the total image which the child may have of himself in certain circumstances. Some one rides into the drive on a horse. One child immediately sees himself as one who can, and undertakes to be taken up beside the rider or to replace the rider. Another child negates the suggestion or hides his eyes to eliminate the horse from his view and remove the necessity to cope with it. Each child may see the horse differently. He doubtless does. The real issue is how does he see himself related to the horse. His image appears always to be one pole of a transaction. The way he sees himself, the horse, and his relation to the horse is a social concept in terms of which he is able to extend himself to a closer relation, or to a remoter one. One child with a peculiarly inadequate self-image could never rest with the simple negation of the relationship of himself with the horse. He busied himself for hours on end with phantasies of torture of the horse, of burying it. These phantasies were exhaustingly elaborate and apparently provoked what seemed empathetic sufferings in himself as his phantasy provided them for the horse. He perspired profusely and underwent facial spasms.

We had formerly realized that the child who believed he was one who could not was predisposed to failure, and that a child who thought that he could, performed beyond his own and others' expectation even when ultimately he could not achieve what he imagined. All our observations tended to increase our faith in our assumption that the more completely the self-image was characterized by canness, the greater the child's progress. We saw that after his own unequivocal experience of success he was able to accept the image flashed back to him from others. We learned not to say to a child, "I'm sure you can if you try."

When he knows that he can't, trial verifies his judgment and makes him still less accessible to the evaluation of others. Instead we say: "Let's see if you can," or "Want to try?" In any case his judgment is honored. Some one else tries and succeeds. Quickly we ask, "You want to try now?" This gives him a second chance to try. The timid often refuse and lack the courage to ask for a second chance. Also in the face of a new experience one type of child fortifies himself against what he considers certain defeat and humiliation. If we pass him quickly, his walls for which experience proved he had no need "come tumbling down." He cannot readily reassemble them. A second request while he is defenseless often succeeds.

We protect our young lives from the experience of failure until they are habituated to success. They need to learn that they cannot do everything, but this is a simple device of teaching which living does for all of us effectively. The habit and attitude of trying is not so easily come by. We might state our prescription in this way.

We like to have the child acquire a basic image of himself as one who *can*—a manner of basic confidence. We like to have him see himself as one needed, wanted, and loved. As he demonstrates his canness, his sense of adequacy increases. As his growing image accepts his adequacy, he becomes more courageous and has less experience of fearfulness. When courage and adequacy are present, he dares give himself to cooperation and has less experience of himself as hostile. An adequate, courageous, cooperative individual has the stuff with which to evaluate himself more highly and thus dares to raise his evaluation of those whom he saw as enemies when he was hostile. Finally then the image of himself leads out toward others in basic confidence. When the negative aspects of fearfulness, hostility, and helplessness were the stuff of his self-image, it led him toward basic anxiety and the consequent neuroses.

For the everyday practices of living with children we translate this assumption into action patterns such as these. We try to resolve all can'tnesses, which are appropriate to size, experience, or ability, into cannesses. Where we can see that they are ultimately appropriate—that is in the direction of actuality—we help the child to tether such purposes with some manner of halter. "When I get big . . ." says Nancy. If it looks remote even to her optimistic eyes, she doubles the adjective: "When I get big, big . . ." We are cautious about the use of the word "impossible." There are so few things which appear impossible and the ingenuity of human kind is always reducing the number. So many things are labeled impossible when actually they are merely improbable, either because no one has viewed them as possible or because no one has been willing to make the necessary effort. We prefer to leave the door open upon the not-yet.

We try never to miss a valid opportunity to hold a positive mirror up to a child. Even a good try can be so labeled. While it is not enough to change a can't into a can, it does help to stabilize a wavering self-image. But unless the tryer is ready to concede success himself, our labeling it for him must fall on deaf ears. Each person can recall those incidents in which his own self-esteem seemed to lean toward inability, but the persistent efforts of one who believed that he could made possible the one more try which carried him past failure to success.

CHAPTER V

Some of the Children Who Taught Us

There is only one subject matter for education, and that is Life in all its manifestations.

—ALFRED NORTH WHITEHEAD

1.

Research in the areas of personality must always lack certain refinements available to research in the behavior of chemicals or the reaction of metals to specific treatment. Matched groups are in actuality never matched when their components are human beings no two of whom are the same and no one of whom remains matched even to himself.

We have selected from Rayswift children a few case histories to show what we have seen as a specialized nurture was provided for children, each one of whom seemed to differ sharply from every other. A few are selected from those whose behavior is still being studied in an attempt to discover with what images of self they meet their days. In these there is little to report as finished but a good deal that may be of practical value in terms of observation undertaken and nurture plans set up experimentally. A few cases have been chosen from the next older group who are in high school now. They have all been with us more than three years and we feel that each has himself well in hand and is leading his life. The quality of their adult life will be known only much later. We have selected three stories from the over twenty-one group.

We have included only one account of a markedly superior child, who has "everything." She is attractive appearing, an I. Q.

185; a rich background in heredity, and practical ability which exceeds our always high expectations of her. When circumstances are too insurmountable, she attributes her failure to handle them to age and size, and announces her intent to do them when she gets "big."

2.

Jimmie was pacing the floor like a caged lion. Round and round, and aimless. Once in a while an unrhythmic jump put him out of step, and then he was back again. Light changed in his eyes and sometimes his lips moved as though he carried on conversations. Real conversation with Jimmie was difficult. His eyes went beyond you. He turned away, or he tried smiles which came and went automatically and without meaning. He could not even tolerate the pressure of a hand on his shoulder.

On one occasion a person came into the room when Jimmie was pacing. Since it was known that direct address was difficult for him, the person said in passing: "I don't know what Jimmie is playing." To this there came the answer: "Jimmie is playing something."

Jimmie is just past nine years. He has a fine body, interesting face, but with a marked habit of closing off its expression when he realizes he is observed. He is eager for food, his intake is normal, and he shows no food idiosyncrasies. He came to us diagnosed as a childhood schizophrenic with a high I. Q.

Directly after Jimmie was born the mother rejoined her husband at an army post. Jimmie's first eighteen months were a history of changes from one camp to another. When the father was discharged Jimmie was eighteen months old. As with so many young couples it was necessary for his family to move in with the maternal grandparents. Another son and his wife moved in soon after and the precocious baby was enmeshed in a close-pressing environment of six adults.

Everyone loved the baby. He was the first grandchild. He was clever, a beautiful child. He chattered like a magpie. He showed a facile memory, repeating songs heard on the radio and stories read to him. With the best of intentions he was exploited as an interesting animated toy. He was taught one trick after the other. He learned long poems without apparent effort. He basked in attention and pampering.

The adults in the household report no unusual behavior until the mother returned from the hospital with a new baby girl. In the course of the next few months the four-and-a-half-year-old Jimmie began to exhibit signs of jealousy, directed against the younger child. The division of attention appeared devastating. He began to show signs of withdrawal. When he was urged back into relatedness, he often panicked. On some occasions he ran into the street naked.

He spent some time in the University Hospital for observation. His schooling had been in the favorable circumstances of a good private school. He had reading ability two or three years in excess of standard. His tastes in literature were for the fanciful, and particularly for Peter Pan.

When the child came to live with us in September and make his first trial in public schools, the second-grade teacher was given a partial history and urged to leave him as far as possible to his own time and ways. His active participation was slow to arrive. He showed a mild pleasure and exhibited no hostility. By the third week he had begun to read when invited. Shortly after, he began volunteering but he remained passive toward all other activities. He used numbers freely by himself. The teacher was advised to use the same methods as with the reading. At the beginning of the sixth week he volunteered correctly concerning some number situation, and after that he passed quickly into adequate participation. All such success experiences were verbalized by all adults concerned and gave him a reflected success evaluation. In all home aspects corrective directions were avoided. When he succeeded in saying the single word "toast" at the table it was provided without more than the usual "please," which is spoken by the nurturer and not demanded of the child even after eight months.

He chose a small girl two years his junior for his friend.

By Christmas he had accepted and carried through a part in the Christmas play. The day following he went to the front of the room on request and told the whole Peter Pan story to his thirty-two eager classmates. These rapid changes in behaviors lead us to wonder whether this child was as sick as was at first suspected.

After seven months the pacing and erratic leaping into the air have subsided. They reappear briefly with visits from parents or grandparents. If he has to be urged to put on a clean garment or to do anything which he did not himself initiate, the pacing begins anew. On two occasions he has panicked over the enforcement of a direction about boots or haircombing and the like. We believe that this child happened upon the visible behaviors of a childhood schizophrenic as a way of avoiding the exhausting attention of the adults about him. He does not lack interest in the people and things about him. He does panic whenever he believes himself involved in these situations. Left to his own devices, he joins in with most things. He is praised for small successes and in general left alone except when he shows signs of wishing to join. He still prefers the less exciting games involving few people and still likes best to read or listen in some degree of isolation. We were early confident that Jimmie's main purpose in life was to escape from contact with other people, whether because of a true childhood schizophrenia, or because he had chosen to hide away from what he fears, as a way of life. We undertook to honor this purpose in all our dealings, so that if this were the answer he had made to his problem, he would learn to find it an unnecessary part of his equipment and eventually lay it down.

This is a technique which to the casual observer is often called "ignoring." Perhaps unskilled observers do not see the real difference that exists. A behavior selected by a child as appropriate for getting the attention of adults shows merely a child drastically in need of the security the attention of adults can give. To ignore his SOS is only to drive him into still more violent search for the attention he must have. Often he is in such desperate need that he accepts the hazard, even the certainty, of negative attention or punishment. To respect such a child's need requires noticing what he is doing and reassuring him that you are paying him attention. In the case of Jimmie respect for his preferences means letting him alone rather than urging him to respond to stimuli which we are sure would be good for him *if* and *when* he is able to support such interest. That *when* only he knows. All we can know is that if he does not of *his* choice pick up what has been displayed before him, he is not yet able to support participation. If he does connect himself, then he is ready, but that decision must rest with him.

We behave toward Jimmie as if these aberrations were his personal preference merely. When the time comes that he may have changed that preference, it will show in a readiness to join.

Early in Jimmie's stay we were betting that our guess was correct, and we wished to test our own theory. The evidence came at Hallowe'en when other children were concerned with costumes and false faces of which they themselves were half afraid. It was obvious he was pleased with his costume, and possibly even glad that his parents had sent it; but he took no initiative to put it on when the other children put theirs on.

"Let me help you put yours on," bridged the gap.

He helped get himself into the pirate outfit in a moment. When he was invited, he responded readily. He was taken before a mirror and smiled in shy approval of his swashbuckling appearance. Then his mask was adjusted.

As if someone had turned an internal switch, the child lighted up. He leaped about in the manner he thought appropriate to a pirate. He slapped the adults on the back and became as open and free with himself in relation to other people as the other children. Behind the mask he felt sufficient withdrawal to dare be himself. For the entire afternoon he outpirated the pirates, apparently draining off both hostilities and self-effacement. The mask became a hindrance and was discarded with its task done.

Jimmie has not in the succeeding months lost this newly acquired assurance. It and the beginning improvement in other subjects than reading are closely related. Recently the child spent a week with the parents and was reported as normally cooperative with his small sister, without the bickering that had been the rule three months earlier. We think we see some return of the withdrawal and certainly of the pacing, which had practically vanished before the visit. We have not been able ever to get any clue to the pattern of the phantasies which appear to be part of his way of life. He is, however, much more interested in small group activities than before this holiday. There is less of the wholesale generosity with toys which marked his first relationships. One had had the impression before that he had little investment in things and cared not at all who owned them. Since the holiday there have been several episodes such as: "That is my top. Only Heidi can play with it." "Those are my candies. When I pass them, you can have some."

He is alert to our varied activities. He watched paperhanging with interest. One can see the questions through the frequently puckered brow, but he is not yet free with basic questions. We try to keep his observation alive by thinking out loud about what is being done and why. He frequently nods his agreement, but such conversation is not directed at him. He participates remotely.

He now asks for toast and is pleased to tell a questioning adult what time it is. It has become academic what actually was the correct first label for him. He is gradually building an image of himself as a cooperative, belonging member of our family, his family, and in a year or two, we believe of the human family which he has capacity to serve well and with insight. How close humanity came to losing him we shudder to remember.

We are trying to win him over to realities from Peter Pan and other fanciful characters. Peter Pan does not serve him as a story. It is a hideout. This he has become insightful about, but he is not yet secure enough to leave it behind him. Animal stories are helping bridge the gap, since there is a real dog in the school, and yet the stories do not demand too much for his identification with the actors. By such slow tactics we expect to help him build an image of himself which does not require phantasy as a retreat from reality, but accepts it as a pleasant occasional diversion.

3.

"Not me. I'm too small," Leslie offered, as someone suggested that he help bring in some wood for the fireplace. One would easily believe by this comment that Leslie had found a first-rate bush to hide behind when he wished to avoid work. It was, however, not that simple. There were places not far beneath his surface behavior where one could see that the child was troubled with the assessment he had made of himself and had most certainly heard in the words and read into the action of the adults who were trying to find out what was responsible for his slow growth.

Leslie is the only child of an unsuccessful marriage. Since he was two and a half, he has been the only child in an overpampering, I'm-mother-and-father-both atmosphere. At nine years two months he has the stature of the average five years six months. Between his seventh and ninth year his recorded growth was one-tenth of an inch.

The mother has given her life to his care. She reports that his growth was always slow. His teachers as well as his mother report a slow reaction to everything except academic matters. He shows an I. Q. of 125, with extra dexterity in manual things. He is interested in electricity and can repair broken plugs, iron cords, and the like. Teachers reported evidence of fatigue and lassitude soon after his school day began.

Leslie arrived at Rayswift on June 29. It had been necessary for him to board a plane in New York, leaving the mother behind and taking the two-hour ride with a comparative stranger. This he was able to do with a maturity and expectation not to be anticipated in one of his years and apparently low vitality.

He immediately made himself at home in our family, choosing the six-and-a-half-year-old girls as his first friends. He is an orderly child, fastidious about the arrangement of clothes and his numerous collections. At the table he picked at his food, drank sparingly and with a curious sucking action rather than deliberate swallowing. It became evident in a few meal times that he not only took in little either solid or liquid, but had developed a remarkable capacity to hold food in his mouth.

It had been his way both at home and here to be excused from the table in the middle of a meal to go to the toilet. The matter had been mentioned to Leslie and no change had taken place. We began to watch. We saw that little food actually was swallowed. He pouched his cheeks like a squirrel and waited his chance to get rid of the food. It was this purpose, rather than the usual bathroom needs, which took him from the table. It showed at once that the necessity was related to the mouth stuffing. He really didn't wish to swallow.

We began to work on the swallowing business since we had had much experience with children who had been fed puréed food too late and had no interest in solid food and an actual aversion to chewing anything. As the child became aware that he must swallow, we began to notice that the throat movements were spasmodic; as one observer said, "He seems not to be able to tell if he will swallow up or swallow down."

We began from another angle since there were apparently causes of this behavior lying too deep to be reached for any conscious cooperation on the child's part. First we modified the diet to include concentrated food values with a minimum of eating effort. We began to free the child from any sense of guilt and helped him to some insight about his necessity to learn to swallow if he wished to grow large enough to use a two-wheeler, which he appeared to desire mildly—though not enough to risk any trials with the small-sized one. He had developed slow eating habits due to all the circumstances cited above. He was now urged to say, "I can't eat this," instead of merely staring at an item of food.

By these techniques we released tensions. This seemed necessary since we were working on the assumption that the difficulty lay on the reflexive rather than the conscious levels. We were also sure that something more than malnutrition was in the picture, for the external signs one would have expected in atrophied muscles, square joints were not in sufficient evidence, if his dwarfism were attributable to poor eating.

As soon as possible—a matter of days—the endocrinological examinations were made. By this time also the cumulative medical reports from half a dozen reputable clinics had arrived, and our observations supplemented with those records gave us a theory. These were the facts.

The birth was normal, instrument-free, and low anaesthetic. Breastfed with good adjustments. On the eighth day, at the doctor's advice, the child was given a bottle, "in case the mother got a cold after she left the hospital."

There is no record of why it occurred; probably the bottle was propped up and the child left. At any rate, Leslie aspirated the milk and came near dying. He was eight weeks in the hospital, tube-fed, in an oxygen tent, while the lungs were dried. It would appear that the deep primal reflexes of swallowing had their own memories of the feeding tube and would retain them for a long time, perhaps forever.

We are working on the assumption that shock such as this child sustained at so early an age may have stopped endocrine action in the growth aspect. This may have been further augmented by emotional shocks which appear to be part of the picture two and a half years later when the parents separated. Thyroid plus pituitary medication has set growth processes actively going.

In his school experience it had been thought wise to keep him in a grade with those of his size rather than of his intelligence and maturity level. We believed this to be a mistake since he was intelligent and mature and actually derived no social satisfactions from classmates his own size. Apparently, seeing such children about him still left him socially alone. We put him into a room where permissiveness and authority are neatly adjusted. He became devoted to it, and with his first successes there the improvement in swallowing appeared. He drinks rather than sucks his liquids. With endocrine medication and heavy vitamins, appetite began to appear. Improvement began in swallowing. No milk is given until the heavily protein diet has been taken. About every six months it becomes necessary to take away all medication for a few days, since at about that interval he has episodes of what he calls unswallowing, without any nausea—an apparently pure rebellion on the part of the stomach to a mechanical overload. In nine months he has grown 2.1 inches and gained 4 pounds in weight.

He takes an active part in his school work, acting in the plays and contributing to the general projects. He has begun to show normal signs in teasing the little girls and on occasion pulling practical jokes intended to cause discomfort to some of the boys in the same age group but of larger size.

In one of the various clinics the child had been given sex hormone which had acted on the genitals alone. He had developed an oversize penis in constant erection. It took five months for the system to clear after this medication had been discontinued.

One need only to have watched the changes in maturity of behavior, in facial expression, and in the play of the great muscles to realize how the "organism acts as a whole." As the growth processes were goaded into action by appropriate medication at the appropriate age, the child's total personality changed too. The babyish look is being replaced by a look of increased maturity. He has become more talkative. He initiates many things in which he was earlier an onlooker. He frequently initiates things for younger children to carry out.

Recently a request was made of two of the nine-year-old boys of normal stature in the presence of Leslie. "How would you like a grate fire and some popcorn? It will take some dry wood and some dry kindling."

Leslie joined the others voluntarily. They donned mufflers and jackets. We waited and watched. Presently all three were back with good nine-year-old loads.

"Look, look how much Leslie's got," one of the others said.

I looked but could see only the peak of a red stocking cap, and a pair of red-mittened hands which appeared to be accompanying a small wood pile out for a walk.

"Good," we cried, "the oldest boy and the biggest load," and in due course fire and popcorn arrived.

4.

"Do you have little children, too?" Jean was inquiring, as he picked at food he had driven a waitress to distraction ordering.

"Yes, we have little children, children your size, and children almost as tall as I am."

"I'm glad there are little ones. I like to hurt them and make them cry. Little girls especially."

Jean was a strange looking little boy. His head was large; his eyes pale blue and never fixed clearly on anything. His garments of expensive cut and texture magnified the immaturity of appearance and behavior. He had been rejected by his mother from birth, although he belonged in a secure economic category where one did not expect to find this.

The father is a fine, sensitive person of Caribbean ancestry and language. Jean is fond of his father, who deals wisely and quietly with him. The mother provides excellently for him materially but permits herself a sharp prejudice in favor of girls, which Jean sensed and which permeated his whole being.

Jean was celebrating his ninth birthday when he came to us. It was arranged this way, as the parents thought, to make his advent propitious as the bringer of a birthday party. We would have preferred to have made the cake here and used it, as we often do, as evidence of general interest for the feted child. We allowed ourselves to be overruled. A week before the child's arrival packages began to come. They mounted into a formidable array and by sheer bulk bade fair to be more a source of jealousy than an argument in favor of the newcomer.

The expensive birthday cake, its size and its decorations, awed our small fry, who disposed of the whole matter by the six-year-old's comment, "It looks bigger, and more beautifuler, but it doesn't stand up so high or taste so good as we usually have."

The packages disgorged toys of an intricacy and design which our children had never seen. To our surprise Jean showed little interest in any of them. When our regulars asked to play with them, they were surrendered to them with a dull kind of acquiescence that was astounding. The child sat most of the time, immobile, but with restive eyes investigating every corner of the room.

When the parents left, his goodbys were equally acquiescent. Left to his own devices, he enlisted the companionship of another child and together they played flying saucers with ten dollars worth of new records. The other children were incensed and let him know what they thought in no uncertain terms. When I inquired if he had not known they were not his to destroy, his answer was that his mother would buy more; she always did, he said, when he broke other people's things.

Flying saucers was a good game for his solitary hostility. Group pressure had sent his companion in crime into retirement; but Jean returned to the game, using the little girls' tin dishes. He was scandalized when he was kept hunting them where he had thrown them and fishing them out of the cold water. He repeated frequently in the hunting process that they belonged to the little girls, and he didn't like little girls. He seemed at a loss at our failure to understand this as sufficient reason for destroying them.

By the end of the first week he seemed confused and clarified at the same time. When it looked as though he might be ready to talk, he was asked if he thought he was going to like being with us. His questions and comments were curiously remote: "Am I to stay here? Am I to go to school here? Don't you do work around here?" One got the impression that the child believed himself a puppet for whom someone would pull strings, and what strings he was mildly interested to know but would not expect to have any part in deciding.

Gradually he began to speak differently, to say "I don't like meat or cabbage" or whatever. Finally he began to ask for string, nails, and things which contributed to his own purposes.

The energy patterns seemed to be low and spotty. He burst into occasional mad rages when he bit and scratched with no clearly defined motivating causes. Endocrine and E.E.G. revealed a slight thyroid deficiency and normal brain waves. We needed to look elsewhere for the origins of these rages.

As swimming time came on, he made a good showing and was quickly released from the nonswimmers' crib. He began to try for the distances which it was necessary that a child accomplish before being allowed to use the rowboat alone. He became prideful of his swimming and handling of the boat.

It had been noted at the first interview that the child was deaf. The reply was that it was a psychological deafness since it was believed that he could hear what he wanted to hear. Others began to see that he was deaf, and as he had no psychological need to be deaf in this setting, we were about to take him to the doctor for examinations when one ear began to drain in a violent fashion. When he was taken for examination, the doctor gave a penicillin shot. It required four adults to hold him. The other ear contained a wax mass too large to come out of the orifice without breaking up. The next shots in the series were taken philosophically and without need of holding. "Now I know what it is," was his laconic comment. The ear difficulty is proving to be serious and may require a hearing aid, yet treatments are making some improvement.

Gradually through the ten months of his stay his social relations with the children began to improve. He has not bitten
anyone for several months. He got so roundly laughed at by the
other children when he fell off his bicycle and bit the tires that
we may have seen the last of that also.

These devices do not seem to be those of a clever child, yet
he gives evidence of more than usual ability in mathematics,
reading and writing. He likes school, makes little difficulty for
the teacher except a too frequent relapse into a lackadaisical attitude about finishing what he has started.

He is a child of few enthusiasms so far, and yet with a shy
yearning to contact people. He was with us more than a month
when he smiled for the first time. He comes up to the people he
prefers and with the least encouragement hugs them in a six-
year-old bear-hug fashion. These expressions are encouraged
and we see a gradual improvement in his ability to support friend-
ships with adults and other children.

During his stay from April to Christmas he was visited once
by his father. This was a profitable experience for him. He was
left alone with the father as much as he liked. Toward the end
of the visit his possessiveness gave way enough to include his
best friends among the children who went with his father to the
store for candy. He spent six days with his family at Christmas.
They expressed themselves as delighted with his friendly behavior, especially with his little sister whom he had hated
cordially, and whom he began to love in absentia through his
past friendship with a precocious girl child here. This girl is
about the size of his sister but several months older.

It was interesting to note two things about the vacations at
home. When he was told the details of the trip home and the
time, there was his usual visible acquiescence, but in the next
two hours there were reports of fighting and destruction not seen
for months. On a chance that he had not realized that the trip
home involved a trip back here, we sought him out and said:
"Aren't you glad you're going to have this nice trip home. You
will be there almost a week, and then you will get back on the
same train, go to bed, and when you wake up you will be in
Detroit, and the car will be there to meet you."

One cannot write the syllable, "Oh," with any of the nuances which his intonation gave it. The bad behavior receded and did not return. We must believe that the child feels safer in this environment. His safety may be made of both the permissive and the authoritative aspects of our regime. He, especially, seems comforted by the clearly stated prohibitions of which there are a few. He leans on them. They are like a fence around a field for him. He has less frustration within the fence and more freedom to motivate himself than he has ever had. He is less pushed around than he has ever been before.

All these apparent contradictions fall into a logical enough pattern if one considers his background. In the beginning the mother, whose income is in the high brackets and whose own one-parent childhood furnished more than the usual pampering and none of the usual frustration, did not want children early in the marriage. If ever there were to be a child, it must be a girl. Ten months after the marriage she bore Jean. She says that he did not interest her. It seemed like an unkind fate that he came to mar the marriage. Hired help took sole care of him for the first two years. Then she became a little interested in him but still resentful of his presence. It may be that he as child, and as boy-child, represents not just himself but the mother's first experience that there were things money could not buy.

At any rate when Jean was a little past three, the mother was again pregnant. The boy was sent to his paternal grandparents, in a strange culture and language, to spend the year. This time fate was kind to the mother. The child was a girl. She was given a name descriptive of the sweet cupids which adorn valentines. That child is a most satisfactory possession. It was into this picture that Jean intruded on his return from his grandparents. It tends to explain why he liked little children whom he could hurt with impunity. It makes it plain why he was puzzled at our not being satisfied with his argument about the little girls' dishes.

The second thing which is noteworthy about the visit home is that, in spite of behaving in a satisfactory way at his own home, he returned to us with a great deal of the old hostility which we hadn't seen for a while. So far it has taken the form of building blocks high and screaming like a banshee as he knocks them over. The rigid tense voice is also with him again. We think it will pass, as in a week's time it has become less habitual.

We think the prognosis for this child is good. His social concern has increased greatly in the nine months. His personal responsibility has increased. He takes better care of his things. He is still over-timid of dark, bugs, and the like. He has grown in generosity under the approval of his sharing. He still collects everything and anything. He has ceased to be light-fingered with other people's things. He recently brought in money he had found on the street and for several weeks no one's pet planes have been found in his drawer. Generally, he had considered it an adequate reason for taking something that he did not have one like it. This aspect of ownership seems well learned now.

The only traces left of his old phantasy-ridden withdrawals show up in tales he tells about Robin Hood or Roy Rogers which tax the fancy of the other children, who laugh them out of court. He is gradually abandoning these tales.

This child will remain in this simpler environment through the remaining years of his elementary schooling, and with the growth we foresee, he will be able at fourteen to enter a fine boy's school of a preparatory type where he can be fitted to his adult needs and to the social position which will be his. We look with some confidence upon his future.

5.

"I will so, won't I? When I get big, big."

A much desired sweet apple hung enticingly out of the reach of small Nancy, an intrepid, often foolhardy tree climber.

Nancy has been, since our first encounter with her at three years two months, a person whose image of herself was most optimistic. She was in no way deterred by the size or stature of any child whom she judged to be dealing unfairly with some one or infringing on her domain. This attitude kept her righting human wrongs all over the place. Had she known the phrase, she would have surely described her domain with Selkirk's phrase. She felt "monarch of all she surveyed."

When Allen's birthday box was being unpacked, it was found

to contain a series of wooden coaches and engine which needed to be hooked together to become a train.

"Let me do it. Allen can't. He doesn't know how."

Without waiting permission, she picked up two coaches out of the box, hooked them together expertly. Apparently reinforced by the ancient grabbing reflex, she then took up the engine, hooked it on, got to the floor with it and cried: "Look at my train run," with appropriate sound effects.

Her marked ability in dealing with any situation while still under three brought her mother to a realization, verified by better trained observers, that here was a remarkable child. The mother, sobered by the evidence of the child's superiority and her maternal responsibility ended abruptly a fifteen year's period as an alcoholic. She stopped and has remained sober now for five years.

For a variety of reasons, the mother, who was alone with the child, sought help more experienced than herself with Nancy's upbringing.

Nancy had already learned to laugh her way out of any situation she judged unfavorable to herself with a disarming and engaging giggle. If, however, this did not serve to divert the situation, the laughter quickly took on a hysterical character. Before she had been two months in the household, she was deferred to by all children under fifteen. "Nancy, see me dive." "Nancy, watch me jump."

There was the usual rivalry to sit next the adult driving the car to and from school. She soon figured out that if she opened the door on the driver's side and invited another child to get in first, she could follow and be just where she wished to be. We watched this without comment for weeks, waiting for some child to discover where this technique led, but no one saw or if they did, they accepted it. It was ultimately necessary, we thought, to cut into this insincerity.

Nancy is short for her age but is in excellent health except for occasional colds which tend to settle in congenitally delicate ears, producing temporary deafness.

She has a vivid sense of humor which derives largely from the recognition of the incongruous. This ability to see and laugh is the most effective tool she has for self-correction. Errors pointed out without this final laugh are often nursed into grudges which eventuate quickly in some subtle nuisance behavior, consciously directed as she has frequently admitted in discussion of them later.

Throughout the four years of her stay we have never been free of the state of being in her which was evidenced in the early device of laughing her way out of a difficulty. As she gets older, it is even plainer to see. Deep beneath her assured-looking, often devil-may-care plunge into some purpose she recognizes as unacceptable, there is a sense of panic that her adults could, just could, let her down. With uncanny differentiation between what is tolerated and the limit beyond which she cannot go, she will desert her cause, attempt to placate whatever gods she immediately recognizes and about face before one of our slower children sees where she is headed.

The apple episode with which this account began was the finishing generalization, which for Nancy was usually verbalized. She was always food-minded, even when her small self was podded out after a generous meal. This sweet apple was plainly out of reach, not only for Nancy but for anyone. Like many an older and more experienced desirer the unattainability made a necessity out of an interesting possibility.

She demanded that her favorite vassal—Arthur, in fact—get it. He measured it with his eye, saw, too, that it was unattainable, and refused. Thereupon she leaped on his back like a tiger, kicking and pummeling him. An observer in a second-floor window had seen the whole procedure, and called Nancy to come upstairs. The trip around the building and upstairs was a matter of seconds. Halfway upstairs she said in a quiet conversational tone: "You want me to tell you why I did that?" An equally quiet: "I saw the whole of it so I know just why you did it, without being told. I'm busy now, so you sit down there until I finish making my bed, and we will talk about it."

In less than ten seconds a bland, melodious small voice was saying, "You know I think you have the nicest room up here!"

This child has been a great education to all of us. Her untrammeled child's incisive analysis clears many a fog and cuts through many a knot. When small Heidi was coming, she announced that the new girl would not like her. We hastened with one voice to say, "Of course she will. Everyone likes you." She made short work of that by saying: "How could she? She doesn't know me." Her first statement proved to be merely an introduction to a plan for helping Heidi to "get to know her" when she did come. It involved explaining to Heidi where the bicycles were to be put at night (although she was no conspicuous observer of her own advice) and allowing her to comb the nylon hair of a newly acquired and temporarily valued doll.

When a school play was in process, she was told to learn her part or she would find some one else taking her place. "Oh now," she said, "they wouldn't do that. They chose me as the best because they knew my mother was an actress in New York and that I would know how." As an afterthought in a truly Nancy-esque way she generalized: "It's the best part, but it isn't much to be a 'ragged old reader tattered and torn.'"

"She will get along all right. I wouldn't worry about her," which we hear so often from casual observers, does not give us much satisfaction. To be sure, she will get along; but will it be along with others, or heedlessly over the top of others? We feel that an organism with such potential can be a hazard as well as an advantage. She has had so little experience with failure that she has not admitted the concept of her non-success into her consciousness. The troublesome thing is that she thinks she can, and then she can. There is so little of coming a cropper that she has no generalizations about it. Temporary frustrations are disposed of as due to her being too little or too young. Their mastery is merely put off.

We think Nancy will go far with her equipment. We are concerned about where or in what direction, but we are not better seers of the future than any others. We are trying to give her some hedging experience with which to modify her image without spoiling its high confidence.

We have chosen her plan of nurture by helping her to question her sportsmanship in talking a smaller or less able child out of some possession. We do not accept unchallenged her favorite answer: "Billy gave it to me." It may be technically true that Billy passed it to her rather than having it wrested from his hands. Hers is a psychological blackjack.

We are arranging her experience, as often as we may, to give her the coveted recognition for willing surrender of items or opportunities to serve other people. "I like to pass the cigarettes and blow out the matches myself, but it's all Arthur can do, so I let him," was a generalization highly prized by us.

We try to lessen the value which derives from difficulty by talking through with her such items as walking an icy log across a ditch. "Of course you could. You can do all sorts of hard things. But just because it's hard doesn't make it worth doing. You could slip like any one else, and then what?"

"A busted head. It's far down there."

Specific situations often bring this type of small generalization and circumstance about her so that she can with increasing accuracy evaluate what it is worth her while to spend herself for. It is harder, or at least requires greater skill so to do, for the questing spirit so often has delicate antennae. If failures and hurts are too severe, effort in these directions is stultified. Then when mature life asks that one take unprofitable risks that some truth may come to birth, the organism cannot take the responsibility. It would be more accurate to say, it cannot give response, for response, the active ingredient in responsibility, must be given. It cannot be taken, though that is the commoner verb to use in connection with responsibility.

Such a personality is delicate. It is easily blunted in sensibility with early hurt or rebuff. Our task is to help Nancy to build her image of herself in such fashion that she can dare anything she thinks is worth daring, and so develop the nuances of those standards of worth that she shall not need to be hurt more often than it takes to stay freshly aware of what pain is, nor weep more tears than are necessary to keep her vision single and her eye clear.

6.

"I wish I could go to school, too." Arthur's gray-brown eyes were clouded and poorly controlled tears welled up, but he did not get the release they were meant to give him. He had the idea, so common in our culture, that maleness precluded the cleansing ministration of crying.

"Someday you can go, I hope, but you need to learn some other things first, and you're doing that right now. You were such a fine person when your daddy took us to dinner yesterday. I think you are learning fast."

"But when am I going to learn to read?"

"Whenever you want to. You can learn any time you want to. I'm glad to help you."

"Right now, I'll get the book."

For the hundredth time the same thing is played over. Able recognition of the words he has mastered—pig, cat, and words of this class, six or seven of them—is in evidence for about three minutes. The first venture with the first novelty and his hands begin waving aimlessly leaping up and down. A dance with the book carried aloft, and the child has escaped from himself beyond his control or mine until the suddenly released energy has played itself out. The best description we can make is that he appears in these moments of desire to have to release his energy in the general direction of his goal, but that release is not, as with most of us, comparable to the lifting of a water gate. It is more as though the dam went out.

It is a frustrating experience. The controls which enable most of us to use some rather than all the energy we have appear to be lacking in Arthur.

It is difficult to be involved with this and not impute to the child a conscious purpose to irritate. Viewed in its entirety it would seem that there is no working mechanism to channel or ration the energy released. He has sufficient insight to realize that he not only is not reading but also is building himself a structure of misbehavior which will finally provoke the adult to some hindering action. When and if this point comes, he gives the same evidence of release and satisfaction one notices in a guilt-driven child who succeeds in getting someone to punish him.

What seems in evidence is the release of total self with little direction available. The flood of energy, which has to go some-where, goes out into action, all action, undifferentiated, undirected to any specific action. The flood then seems to gain momentum as though some gravitational force pulled out more and more. Experimentation has shown us that if we can stop the gap with a stern word or refocus attention with a rap on a table or a grasp of the arm, the flood stage is stopped; but it helps little, if any, in the attempt to turn the energy into a designed path.

We make further observations. Does this happen with self-initiated actions? To our surprise it does not. A self-designed project to "plumb" the sandbox has kept him unremittingly busy, with a fine articulation of his hands in putting cinches on threaded pipe-length. These often required several tries to get the joint turning evenly on the threads. In fastening wires around poles to put a new plug on a lamp, there is the same tense activity, but the energy moves into action evenly and without waste. Paper-and-blocks construction hold attention and are manipulated without panic.

These observations lead us to the conclusion that the machinery for metering his energy exists and can work when other things are right. But which other things, and what constitutes right?

The history gives some background. The child was taken by Caesarean section. The mother for unknown reasons suffered shock and the child's animation was suspended. In wartime shortage of help, oxygen was not immediately available, and possibly eight minutes elapsed while the baby was without it. By this time the infant was, as his physician father described it, "more dead than alive." Finally he did take up breathing.

He was taken home from the hospital by the parents and the difficulty was believed to be over. However the mother who had borne three other children noticed his unusual lassitude and lack of crying. She went to work with a kind of frenzy. She taught him to cry by imitation. She tried every type of stimulation she could devise to get him to make responses. She taught him to talk by breaking down the sounds in a word and finally helping him combine them by imitation. In the light of the effort expended in those earlier days his near-normal abilities and concepts are amazing, even miraculous.

He walked late, and early gave evidence of slow maturity. By the age of four he had developed an exploratory interest in his backyard and in the neighborhood. He was the one child who fell, who got badly hurt by little accidents, whose front teeth got knocked out, whose leg was gashed by falling from a tree. No recorded observations are available from this period, and it is hard to guess whether this took on something of an accident-proneness, or whether a judgment less developed than normal may have tempted him to try things which a more normal child would have judged impossible or too hazardous.

It was observed early that he fared better—that is behaved more normally—if directed with brief clipped terms and held to a somewhat high regimentation. It appeared that the child had neither the mechanism nor the skill to use freedom. Choices among toys and foods were difficult. He tried indiscriminate attempts to avoid the effort of choice, in favor of taking anything and everything. His greed approximated that of a starved child, although he had never known food denial or malnutrition of chemical origin. There is no reasonable explanation for the greed with the possible exception of the mother's more than average interest in food as a symbol of success over circumstance.

In recognition of the need for regimentation, the child was sent to a private school where discipline was strict. The people in charge were not told of his difficulties or his inabilities. They undertook to do with him as with normal children, reporting indifferent success but not failure. His adjusting behavior was slow moving, and he fatigued unduly.

The next semester, when teachers were told about him, his deterioration became more marked. No facts are known about his handling for those few weeks. Our guess is that the child either heard of his inferiority or experienced it in action, and came by some sort of deep conviction, of which, if he could verbalize, he would say: "I can't do what they want. I'm not as smart as the rest. I will clown and make myself laugh at me, and perhaps others will laugh, and I need not admit that I can't. They will think I could if I tried, but I won't try, and I won't because I and they will see that I really can't."

This is conjecture. We arrange his circumstances so that he has continuous stimuli to do something, and when efforts cannot be sustained, the stimulus is withdrawn without negative comment.

His vocabulary is extensive and accurate. He ties into conversations by question rather than statement. Gradually the response, "You know. You tell me," brings the desired interrelation. He has wide interests in almost everything. He asks intelligent questions, and often checks them through with such statements as "then it would break, wouldn't it?"

He expresses and is hilariously amused with incongruities: "What if someone swallowed a horse?" a few minutes after a suggestion to put lighter loads on his fork. He has high aesthetic abilities. He, of all the children, is mindful of sunset colors and opening flower buds. He creates beautiful things with clay, paint, paper, and has joy of them. He frequently requests coloring books, but soon resents the guiding lines and responds, not with poor coloring, but with violent broadside strokes, as though he said, "I do not care that I cannot do this, but see how big I show that I don't."

He is tender of illness or hurt in others but also overestimates his own scratches and cuts. He demands bandaids for every one. He shows insecurity about sleeping. He is never satisfied until he understands the sleeping arrangements for guests, and on overnight trips he worries about the coming night until reassured.

On a recent visit to his distant home he behaved in his most exaggerated manic manner, seeming to be putting his parents' concern with him to every possible test, yet as soon as he was five minutes in the car for the return trip, he had quieted to normal and slept for hours. When he woke, it was with the pettishness of a teething baby. He went into a hysteria of tears and laughter when he was fully awake. He is usually, as are most brain-damaged we know, in need of less sleep than normal children, yet he slept hours again the next day.

In spite of his handicaps and his intolerable teasing of other children when he cannot handle his part in games, he is still loved by those children who most often suffer from his antics. When he is in serious trouble for destructiveness they are likely to shield him. Most of his destructiveness stems from ill-advised curiosity. On one occasion, someone asked a precocious younger child: "What is wrong with Arthur?" She answered indignantly, "There isn't anything wrong with him. He just left part of his brains where he used to live."

He is a bit feminine in his tastes. He likes to wear necklaces and bracelets, especially those he has made himself. He likes to wear an apron and fuss about the kitchen. He can do a number of small chores adequately. Outside he is interested in gardening and has some skill in simple operations. He admires new garments, once noticed a new patent leather purse some one was carrying with the remark: "I like that purse, but better with your patent leather shoes than the ones you have on now."

Whether as a part of his need for intensified experience, or a part of a native sensory pattern, he is one who must touch to understand and is in constant need of physical contact with his adults. He sits on laps as often as possible, although he is a little tall for his ten years.

He is interested in music. He listens to records, has fondness for marked or exotic rhythms. So far we have not been able to hold his interest in tapping out tunes on a xylophone, where he need only match color to color. He is easily offended by any cacophony.

He has an inordinate interest in sex matters, although he is well and unemotionally informed. He knows that a line of vulgarities which he sometimes spouts has nuisance value. He apparently believes it excellent conversational material. He often draws a man sitting on a toilet—so he says—and laughs hilariously as though it were an excellent joke. We do not know from what source these behaviors stem, nor do we have much success in replacing them.

The parents' great emotional investment in him blinded them to the damage he was doing to the older children in the family. His foolish behavior, likely to be on the side of exhibitionism and vulgar talk, was hard on the adolescent pride of his siblings. The destructive results of his curiosity were hard on the sisters' dolls and toys. His occasional visits home are still difficult for everyone including Arthur himself.

He is much more loved by his present companions than by his siblings. He is a definite member of the group, even if often connected as a nuisance. He is evaluated by the others as one who needs to be looked after, and each is warmly resigned to his share.

He has definite handicaps which we believe are due to emotional causes. We believe that a part of his inferiority lies in his convictions of it both from early schooling and from self-derived judgments based on other people's actions rather than their words. We have some hope for his future, which we think may bring some degree of usefulness in a controlled situation. His interest in plants and his concentration on their growth looks like a good lead now. His parents anticipate developing a farm property with greenhouse, to which they will ultimately retire, as giving scope for these interests. The hand work gives satisfaction since those manipulations of a repetitive nature can turn results without much recourse to higher level cortical activity. This, we believe, is useful—and not as a way of passing time, as many advocate. Time neither crowds nor troubles the less able whose pursuits are not articulated with commonly defined social and industrial standards. He can wait, and he can putter about on jobs of his own devising.

As his maturity opens a little wider system of values, there are more goals worth spending himself for. In his three years here we have seen this mount sufficiently to guarantee that the mechanism of evaluations is in function, even if on a simpler level and a reduced rate. We use the single goal-defining label of "fine person," rather than labeling as "good" or "bad" behaviors upon which he is not yet equipped to pass ethical judgments. He does value having people like him, and undesired behavior is discussed as "the things that make it hard for people to like you." When people like you, they want to give you things and do nice things. By this technique he has learned to go shopping without handling "the storekeeper's things" or asking to buy. In the beginning each success resulted in being allowed "to select what you would like. You have been such a fine person it makes me want to do something nice for you."

The next step was to invite him to go in the car. "I have to buy some things, but we will not be able to buy anything for you this time. I will be glad to have a fine person like you for company, and you will enjoy me, if I can be a fine person too." This procedure is now at the stage where Arthur asks as he gets in, "Will we get something for me or is this a fine person trip?" This procedure is slow, but we think rewarding. The time is gradually lengthening, and so long as he is the only child involved he is successful for over two hours. With another child present it is unpredictable. Possibly the effort incident to relating to another youngster exhausts him emotionally sooner than with an adult.

Part of the progress made may be attributable to changed education and different nurture ideation; but part is also attributable to the correction of a congenital thyroid deficiency, which was discovered only at seven and has since put the pituitary into fuller action, and for some not understood cause now lets the thyroid function satisfactorily without any medication. All other physical development is normal for his age and inheritance.

7.

"You have been up since seven and it's now eight-thirty and you are just coming into breakfast. There just isn't any reason, is there?"

"Yes," said Red, in his considered drawl.

"Well, what?"

"I never hurry."

How completely Redlike this was. A complete law unto himself, getting under way in the morning had required the services of one extra person from babyhood until he came to us. He was now fifteen and had been six years with us. It was frequently necessary for us to look at his initial photograph in order to keep our faith and go on.

Red was a foster child. Data about his birth were scarce. The birth had been difficult. There was a great deal of damage to motor areas at that time. Teachers found him so disturbing to other pupils at school that he was denied the public schools at the second-grade level. His queer-sounding voice was irritating and "he didn't act even as though he heard" what he was asked to do. He was a queer-looking child. A milk-white skin was generously sprinkled with freckles. He was long in the torso and short in the legs. His long, slender, artistic hands moved constantly like antennae. Pale blue eyes looked through thick glasses, and over his ear hung the telltale cord of a hearing aid which had been purchased when one of the many private schools which had taken but passed him on in the previous years had found it necessary.

The first teacher was right. He not only acted as if he didn't hear. He didn't—not even his own speech, to any marked extent. All this topped by the flame from the top of his head had made him the butt of child jokes. He was sensitive and frequently in tears. He sold toys and valuable things for a few pennies whenever he caught the children in good humor. He was said to "have no money sense." We think he merely paid big prices for what he thought he could get in no other way.

When he came to us he found a group of children accustomed to people who had difficulties and minded to help them. Our experience changed the attitude in which we were trained, namely that children were cruel to each other. We know now that they are not cruel, though they are often ignorant. When they find out why the other is different they busy themselves being helpful instead of being what people have called mean. So no one plagued Red. He had a birthday party soon after his arrival to which the parents came. They were astonished at the way two weeks had cemented him into the group in a friendly fashion.

As we began our routine observations of Red we discovered that there were other things besides the obvious handicaps, although those were numerous enough to account for almost everything. There were, for example, six or eight times a day, wild rages, which resulted in head bumping and beating with any article handy. Some of these were traceable to frustration that the crippled hands did not do the fine things he bade them. Some came from his inability to carry without spilling, dropping, and the like. His rage was never directed at anyone but himself. Certain growth anomalies, queer proportions and square joints, led us to check both with E.E.G. and with endocrine examination. The E.E.G. was normal, but pituitary shortage was indicated.

He was immediately put on thyroid for six weeks and pituitary for nineteen months. During medication his proportions changed. His legs lengthened. His arms, a bit paddle-like and carried pendulously, fell into symmetry. At sixteen when he left us he was a finely proportioned five feet ten and one half.

His educational history begins with his refusal by the schools in the second grade. Two years of different private schools followed, and two years of tutoring when he was thought ready for the seventh grade of public school. He did excellent work both in seventh and eighth up to the last weeks in each. He either ran out of energy or was bored, or both, and was passed in terms of the preceding twelve weeks. He is now in a special school in preparation for college. He has an I.Q. of approximately 170, is scientifically minded, and shows high potential for ultimate success in a limited field.

His hearing, which is only 20 per cent of normal, makes it difficult to teach him by any oral process. He learns quickly from printed page and from radio (turned to high volume).

While he was being tutored at home there was also evidence of easy fatigue and need for frequent change and novelty. A set of subtraction examples in borrowing were being checked, preparatory to the tutor's arrival. The first sixteen were perfect. The last eight were not only wrong, they were fantastic.

"What happened here?" we inquired.

"Oh, that—you see I get tired doing these your way. You always borrow one. When I borrow, I borrow five."

While he was under medication the endocrinologist said: "Wish we could get some exercise for those long muscles. Something like golf. Trouble is if you send him to play golf, it soon gets into competition. The extra excitement does more harm than the play does good."

We went into a huddle and came up with a pair of cheap golf clubs and a few balls. Red and his pal were each given a club and some balls, with the understanding that when the balls were lost, there would be no others. It was also suggested that we as kids had done all right with tin cans battered into the semblance of a ball. All summer long these two swung and hit, with nothing and no one with whom to compete. This accomplished a great deal. That fall Red began to write, even to draw. He became skilled in carrying dishes. He chose table clearing for a job, and shortly before he left, he said: "Do you remember before how I couldn't carry out my empty porridge bowl without getting milk on the ceiling? Well, now I can serve the slipperiest dessert you can make without spilling it."

The last statement was true; the first slightly overstated.

His personal history is interesting. He met strangers well and always began conversations, although he was well pleased to read or listen to his radio by himself. He might well have been expected to show a pseudo-paranoia as so many of the deaf do. We believe that this was early forestalled by his inclusion in every activity: giving him responsible shares in picnic preparations, in packaging frozen vegetables, and every communal task we could find. Everyone took pains to see that he heard all that was said. A message was often relayed through three or four children until some one near could speak into the hearing aid.

Only rarely did he use his handicap for a shield. Once while we were working on the temper outbursts, a visiting two-year-old put on a tantrum when her mother refused her a second dessert. Red was scandalized at such behavior. He was so verbal about it that someone finally said: "You see, Red, people don't really enjoy seeing people throw temper tantrums like this."

His eyes sought the speaker's face to verify his suspicion. He quickly turned off his hearing aid, as he said: "I don't intend to listen to any such talk!"

What his future will be is anyone's guess. He has grown normally. He is socially competent. He is skilled in reading ability and background. He is still slow, opinionated, an easy mark for barter or purchase if he is anxious for the goodwill of the purchaser. He has a good deal of insight, and some pessimism about his future. "Those are wonderful ships," he remarked as he looked at a picture, "but with my handicaps I can never get in the navy. Do you think people who are deaf ever get anyone to marry them?"

His keen humor and his freedom from paranoic slants offer the greatest hope for his maturity.

8.

"When I couldn't read, I didn't think I would ever get through high school, and all the rest of the family went through college."

"Don't forget there is still your brother Bill in the senior class too."

"That doesn't count yet. He will get through because he is smarter than the rest of us."

It is possible that an unbiased senior English teacher in high school might still not think much of Helen as a reader, but for us who have seen this girl move from a dejected, over-tall, lip-hanging drain on her parents and friends to a bright, alert, socially acceptable, happy eighteen-year-old, she is one of the seven wonders.

We were discouraged with Helen when she came. Scion of a distinguished family, she had a tradition hard to live up to, and the purposeless sag of the fine young shoulders made her look to us like one of the worst—namely one who knows by her own convictions that she is barred from achieving what she thinks others expect of her.

We were not alone in our discouragement. The pediatrician who had taken care of her from birth had advised an institution for Helen. The pediatrician had his evidence too, but it was a piecemeal judgment made from seeing the child in the office or on rare occasions in bed with various ailments. At five Helen had suffered an episode in which she had fallen unconscious in what appeared to be an epileptiform seizure. The Mayo Clinic made a diagnosis. E.E.G. was not clear. The kietogenic diet then in use was followed for a brief period. No repetition of the seizures occurred.

The child was described as aggressively hostile, particularly against the younger brother who was pampered by the other members of the family. Rages, not clearly defined in origin, made medical people further concerned. She entered school a year late as a result of medical care, and never made a good adjustment. We were prevailed upon to take her at her fourteenth birthday. She had just returned from a summer camp, where she had learned to swim. She was entered in the village high school in the ninth grade. She had failed the eighth grade, and in the small town in which she lived, the younger brother would have been in the same room.

It was explained that this child had severe handicaps, could not yet read easily, and might not succeed. We arranged for a school program without mathematics, of which she was in terror. The first semester was hectic. The adjustment was not easy for her, and the course to follow was not clearly defined. After the first report card, when she was given the minimum passing grade, we began a systematic program of upgrading the reading. Our methods, however, had nothing to do with the mechanics of reading. She was built up in every way possible, and there are many ways with any child, if one's intent is to find what is right about the child rather than what is wrong.

"How do you find out a word you don't know?" she inquired. A bit of simple phonics was introduced. She was asked to read a story to the smaller children. The book was first-grade level, and we all kept out of sight, but not out of earshot. The pictures helped the meaning, and a six-year-old who could read did some correcting. One of us entered the room to pick up something. The reading stuttered to a hopeless pause. We went out and it began again.

She was thanked for reading by the adult, and it was pointed out what a help it was to have another older person to read to the little ones. She took this over as her task, and we hardly knew when she learned to read schoolbooks. Kindly, patient acceptance of her about-to-be success has got her close to graduation in her senior year, with only one failure in her first semester. She now gets A's in sociology and passing grades in other subjects. Her graduation is a certainty.

Several interesting sidelights have come to the fore with Helen. Her room has remained a major trial both to us and to her. The disorder is complete. We have investigated all our clues and used all our persuasions. She has been called home from school, when it was necessary to walk back. She has been docked on her salary for the extra labor of others in cleaning the room. The room was designed, papered, curtained, and so forth in the first place in complete accord with her taste.

Once she figured she had not closet space enough. The wall was opened and a new closet provided, but the garments did not jump on the hangers. We suspected they wouldn't, because the dirty garments had not leaped into the new hamper, nor the clean ones into the drawers. They hung fantastically from the edge of the drawers.

Finally it began to come out. "Why is it," she was asked for the hundredth time, "that you can't keep a better room? You like us. We like you. You know how often we both have been humiliated by it."

"I don't know, myself. I always try to do what you want me to do. I know it ought to be different, but when I start to clean it, I can just hear my mother threatening to tell my dad and have him slap me, and I get stopped."

The mother does have a whining voice. She is devoted to her children. It had been her custom to confine her discipline to threats and require the father to punish the child for misdemeanors which occurred out of his sight. The child hangs all her dissatisfaction with herself and with life on her mother, and plainly resents the mother's part in spoiling the relation with the father which might be described as both fearful and frantically concerned to please him.

The child had interpreted her early difficulties as rejection. The apologetic note in voices as she was compared with siblings fed these convictions. When she was small the otherwise dissatisfied mother, as the child saw it, did give her gentle handling and care whenever she soiled herself or later became excessively dirty at play. When her own personal pride deprived her of this satisfaction and she gave up the practice, she transferred the mess elsewhere, and since we all thought that the simple logic was to require her to clean it up, she was deprived of this symbol of parent's care she did not quite trust without evidence. Now that we know, we have stressed still farther her great worth to us, our pride in her accomplishment, and guardedly pointed out that it was time- and strength-consuming for older people to put it to rights. We are seeing some improvement.

A few weeks ago she returned from a weekend at home. She was seething like a kettle.

"Did you have a nice time at home?"

The kettle boiled over.

"They made me spell all the words on the signboards going and coming; and at every meal for dessert I had to do problems in my head."

We didn't much blame her for being mad, even though she also knew that they meant well. We have tried to keep Helen happy and given her every facility with which to build up her image of herself. She is minded by background and inclination toward marriage and children. We have sought the successes which go with homemaking and skill and interest in child care. She developed a fine outgoing empathetic concern for children who were ill or had handicaps.

From the beginning we assumed that this girl had fine human potentialities, and that academic achievement, if it came at all, would lie the other side of a tremendous lack of confidence in her perception of herself. She was asked her opinion about the progress of other children, and aside from a certain gruffness which she put on like a garment to prop up her new sense of importance, her judgment was excellent. Spending herself for manifestly less able people helped in her image building. Her judgment was valued also with the children, and when Helen said, "You know very well that what you were doing wasn't right, and you did it anyway. Stop your nonsense and do better," it carried more weight than the word of older people. No blame or bright expectation was ever voiced about report cards. When she said it was better, we were mildly glad. When it wasn't, nothing was said. As we continued to be undisturbed, she lost her fear of grades, and ceased to remark on unfairnesses in teacher judgment. From telling the stories of historical novels ancient history began to come alive for her. "Those Greeks and Romans were people and fell in love and died like real people."

Books and magazines of all levels are about. She began reading for pleasure rather saccharine stories in the housewife's-type magazines. She soon discovered that a continued story was only a novel in small bites. Next she began bringing home paper editions with lurid covers. When she said one was good, one of us read it and offered one of our favorites as like it. She still comments on how much trouble she made herself by not learning to read, and has by now read a great deal and has a gradually maturing taste, but it does not include the time-honored classics, which have been too carefully dissected by a well meaning but curiously insensitive English teacher.

Now she talks college and a nursing course. We are mouse-quiet and appear only mildly interested in what she has to say about it. Some of us have great expectations for a useful and happy life for her, but we are biased in the direction of *optimism*. "She is born but she isn't dead," is an old midwest way of saying nobody knows. We do know that she is not likely to need any institution as her doctor prophesied. She is a fine, sensitive person, eager to marry, have children, and "do right by them." We could wish to live long enough to see what measures she would use on her prospective daughter in teaching her to keep an orderly room!

9.

"Maybe, then, I could be the bush expert," Larry was saying. He looked up at me with his tangle of yellow hair covering his face like a sheep dog, but the glint of the blue eyes and the twigs and dead leaves in his hair were reminiscent of a modern Pan with clippers.

"Wonderful," I exclaimed, and it *was* wonderful how his judicious trimming of the old monstrosity of a honeysuckle bush had restored its symmetry and left its aging branches with some of its younger grace.

This was four o'clock of Larry's first day with us. He had arrived just before lunch. Extra large for his age, he walked with the curious hunching over-tall adolescents are able to achieve without breaking. His hands were finely built and articulated, and a glint of fuzz that bespoke a precocious maturity shone along his jaws.

Most disturbing were the quick glances he shot here and there about the house, and particularly at the other young people at his table. Directly after lunch the family council met. This council meets on occasion whenever a child feels a thing needs talking through, or an adult feels the need of the advice of the young.

Either can call it, and it brings together everyone living under our roofs. It had been called this time by one of the older girls with the idea that since it was the first day of summer vacation there would be more time to earn extra money for those who wished to do so. But they would need to know what the jobs were.

Larry sat in as a new member. There was the usual clearance between the young workers and the adults. The gardener spoke of things he would need help with. There was a lot of lawn mowing, some weeding in the raspberries, and the shrubbery was getting out of hand. The fence around the dogpen needed mending. The housekeeper mentioned walls that would need washing, children's furniture which needed repair and paint, as well as the routine of loading and unloading the dishwasher, helping young fry to learn to make their beds. There was certain policing of the outdoor dining room which seemed always to need something in the way of pickup, and the weeding of the swimming beach. The older children felt that these latter two jobs concerned everybody and ought not to be included in the jobs for which we get paid. One remarked that weeding in the water was hard enough work to get paid for. Another said that was not the point. The point was that it belonged to the house and the family, and should be done because we lived here. The argument was climaxed with the ambiguous: "If you had to go clear to Metropolitan Beach and pay every time you swim, you wouldn't weed that beach for free, but this is ours."

Finally each had chosen his task. Wages had been decided upon; adults agreed to post charts as reminders. The meeting ended with someone's saying, "Maybe Larry doesn't understand about this. Do you?"

"Well yes, I guess I do, but I see everyone has a job to earn money but me. Couldn't I have one, too?"

An adult spoke up to say: "Certainly, but perhaps you will want to look around first to see what work you would like to do?" "No, ma'am," was the reply. "I like to do every work, and what I don't know about, I can learn."

"Could you trim shrubs?" I inquired. "It's a little hard, you know."

"I don't mind hard. I'm strong," he countered eagerly.

"That isn't the kind of hard I mean. I'm sure you are strong. What I mean is that after you cut off a piece you can't put it back on."

Larry hesitated a second, and then said, "I could cut off what I am sure about and ask about the rest."

It was agreed that this would be good to do and the meeting broke up. For two hours, I was called every few minutes, and it became increasingly clear that he was cautious and persistent and careful, as well as having a fine eye for symmetry. Finally, he was finished except for the monstrous honeysuckle. I said: "Do what you can with it. I don't even know how it should be."

So it was that Larry became the bush expert for the place. It is a unique label, we think, but it worked the first miracle with one whose image of self so desperately needed an addition in which he could see himself as one whom people liked and trusted. This we recognized, but all we really knew about how to do that difficult job was for him to come to love and trust people. This proved to be a task.

We had been alerted by our first look at him to a precocious physical maturity. Enormous physical strength, two and a half inches taller than standard. The meager records then available gave us no information except that his tonsils were out and he had already had measles. Verbal report said that he was possibly schizoid, since he withdrew into himself so frequently, was rather antisocial, avoided group activities. He was given to violent outbreaks of temper which came without apparent reason or justification. He was slightly artistic and had been given a sketchbook. His intelligence was possibly a little low, since he couldn't read. He had never been delinquent, although he had often been associated with delinquents.

Little was known of his own father. He had been driven out of his mother's house at five by a drunken and cruel stepfather. Since then he had been in and out of boarding houses and was complained about by boarding mothers because "when he got mad he wouldn't wash or change until he was smelly." For reasons which we do not know that had become his fighting device, and it was an effective one. It may well be that one of the women in whose house he lived had frequently called him "a stinker," and with the consistency of adolescence he may have decided to live up to his label.

Two procedures seemed indicated. One was to begin by every possibility we could find to give the boy evidence of concern with him, and to compliment every good behavior. We say among ourselves, "bookkeep" every good thing. Unless such are underscored by comment, the fund of successes in living may seem less than it is, since most of us find it easier to locate the few things wrong than to capitalize on the many things right.

The second procedure involved investigating hunches on the simple practical level. We have learned to look, not only to find out whether a child is dirty but also to see if he has what it takes to keep clean. A person who has mastered general cleanliness will recognize and report inadequacies. One who has not either does not recognize them or exploits them under criticism.

Precocious maturity usually means trouble—physiological sometimes, and sometimes what might be called social—since his precocious size gives the observer an unconscious expectation of maturity and experience out of proportion to the actual state. Since time is of the essence of maturity this is not a fair expectation of the large young.

A checkover of his clothes revealed garments enough to justify the statement that he was adequately clothed. But almost everything was a great deal too small. New things were necessary and the money provided by the state was inadequate. The Junior League funds covered the discrepancy between state allowance and our fees. A fifteenth birthday was coming up, so clothes made up a large part of his numerous packages. Children who have lived under A.D.C. or other child-care agencies usually suffer from the scant as well as impersonal aspect of the provision. Enough is not therapeutic. Large doses of more than enough are required. Numerous packages for birthday or Christmas are important. Enough, or the one good gift which frugality would indicate, does not fill the need in these cases. Enough merely meets need, with the sense that when these are gone new needs will recur. Too much from this point of view acts like a medicine. He had a lot to unwrap. He had four layers to his birthday cake. There was thicker frosting, and more decorations. Everyone gathered at his table to sing happy birthday, and their singing came true.

All these small things helped to fill the emptinesses, but the holes were deep! The first weeks went smoothly, but as always such studied good behavior had to subside at times. He got mad at adults who had to remind him to do those things he so often had promised with a hearty "sure I will." As fast as possible and while first things were going on, we were planning for physical examinations. Larry slept too much. He sat too long and too often in a kind of trance over his empty sketchbook. Medical examination revealed what had been suspected—an over-active pituitary, a sex development far in excess of his age. An excessive need for sugar became evident and made some analyses necessary, which were nonetheless negative.

In spite of a reading disability he was able to bring home passable grades in the seventh grade. The teacher missed him greatly when he was occasionally absent that fall. Trips were made to the eye specialist, as we undertook to get at the reading disability. School books had been purchased for him. New shoes were in order. Without any attention called to it on our part, Larry began to be concerned about the money being spent for him. He did not have much left from his earnings for more than his once-a-week trip to the show and the cheap model planes in which he was interested.

One day an adult went to pick the children up at school. Larry was not there. An hour later he returned, saying that his teacher had had him stay to help with spelling. It passed without comment until supper was over when it was confided to me that this could not be true since the teacher left early each Thursday for a class at the university. An occasion of privacy was arranged without fuss and the adult inquired, "I am surprised that you felt it necessary to lie about where you were after school. Have I ever said no to you about anything?"

A somewhat surprised, "No, and I have often wondered about it."

"You do not have to hear no, because you are always sensible in your requests. Do you remember last week when you came and asked to go after airplane glue, I said—do you remember what I said?"

"Yes. You said you have good judgment. You needn't ask to go anywhere. But, it is nice that you came because I do need to know where you are in case of a phone or a visitor."

"That's right. So why did you need to lie this time? I set great store by how honest you are."

"You spend too much for me. I don't belong to you. I went to see about a paper route, so I can earn."

"And did you think I would not let you do that?"

"I didn't know. Will you?"

"I see no reason against it, but it is like going into business. Maybe we ought to talk it through before you decide. If it makes you late for supper, for example, that cuts you from your dish job, as well as making trouble for the kitchen."

He took the route. The money was ready and left for the collector each week. People called and thanked "that nice boy" who puts the paper inside the door in bad weather. Everything seemed fine, and vigilance was relaxed. Christmas was coming on. He sold Christmas cards. His pleasanter, no longer withdrawn ways made him a good merchant. Since the accounts seemed to be satisfactory it slipped our attention that his inability to write must make him trouble. We investigated when we did think of it, and discovered that he had drawn a picture of every purchaser's house rather than writing down names.

At this time he was going to Detroit weekly by himself for eye treatments. On one occasion—it was collecting day—the worker in his house discovered that the thirty-six dollars for cards, which belonged to the collector, was missing and no envelope had been left for last week's papers. When he came back, he displayed a pocket full of money, and readily agreed that it was dangerous to take it to town. The collector had been forgotten.

A few days later two of us left for a brief trip. The second evening away, the person left in charge heard a shot, and went to investigate. Here was Larry with a gun shooting across the lake. In a well-handled discussion Larry willingly surrendered the gun, "until I returned." The card money was again missing but it was not immediately clear where it had gone.

The gun was the result of the missing money. It had been brought home piecemeal, buried in a field, and only now dug up and fitted together. What did a surreptitious gun and misappropriated funds have to do with all this? Long discussions followed. The paper dealer was interested and helpful. He took some blame to himself that he had not required records, but since the money had always been right, he had been lax.

"But that isn't how it should be," Larry added.

"What I wonder," the paper dealer inquired, "is what did you do with the rest of the money? Your second-hand gun only cost sixteen dollars."

"I don't know myself. I always wanted enough candy bars, and just once before I tasted a banana split," was the answer.

It was true. Within a period of three days the boy had devoured twenty dollars' worth of candy bars and banana splits!

The newspaper dealer was paid off and the boy signed a note with us to be worked off. Perhaps no other thing did more to convince him of our real interest in him. We explained the mechanics of sugar, the hazards of its overuse, and agreed to give him larger or double desserts if he would budget himself on purchased sweets. This has been rigidly adhered to. The passion for sweet—this time it was no worse a thing than overstimulated taste buds and live taste memories—has subsided under temperance. Plenty of candy and ice cream were made legally available, and that one was over.

More than a year later, the local hardware man called to inquire if I intended to have Larry get a gun. He had asked to have one put aside and had made a down payment. We suggested that the merchant hold it until I got expert male advice. Without questioning about the gun, we inquired of Larry: "It's right in the middle of hunting season and we have wondered if you thought you should have a gun." He brightened visibly and said: "Gosh, I'd like to have a gun. Are you going to let me?"

"I have been discussing it with someone who's had a lot of experience with guns. He thinks you should have one if you are willing to learn how to use it correctly. I can't see why anyone wants a gun, but I'm not a man."

Still no comment on the one put away. "I've invited this person out for this weekend. He will bring a gun and teach you. If he finds you can learn to use it carefully, he will go with you and help arrange for you to buy it in partial payments if you like."

"I got good credit. I paid for my razor and for my bicycle light. He says I got good credit, and that it is very important to have good credit."

"What were you using your credit to buy?"

"I had him put away a gun, but I know I was nuts. I knew I couldn't have it—account of last time."

"This doesn't have anything to do with that. This depends entirely on your ways of doing tomorrow—and if then you are to have a gun, I would like it to be a good one." His learning was good. He got his good gun, paid for it on time, and has been able to abide completely by rules he helped make about when and where he might use it. He has given a good account of himself twice on hunting trips in the north woods, the only boy with groups of men.

The difficulty about keeping clean went deeper than the need for clothes with which to keep clean. It was necessary to explain at length and several times that our washing machines would rather deal with three pairs of soiled underpants than with one pair worn a week. This helped. But it remained difficult to get his hamper in to the laundry, until he began to help a younger newcomer in the same building to get his in. Now it is reduced to about what I would expect of seventeen.

It had been our method to say, when all milder treatment was fruitless, "Look, two people have been all day making a fine meal for all of us. It doesn't seem quite right to spoil their meal by having you at the table smelling objectionable. Clean up before you come in." This usually brought him in clean and fine. One day, however, when some other matter had gone badly, he resorted to the old trick of getting too dirty. The usual procedure did not work. After due time elapsed, a visit to his house confirmed what was anticipated. There he was glowering and mumbling. "What's your trouble?" was asked. "No clean jeans," was the laconic answer. "Then they are in somebody else's drawer. I'll find them." They were produced and as the adult was about to leave, he said to Larry: "Funny thing that anyone who can swim as well as you do should be so afraid of water in small quantities!"

"I am not," he answered, but in the voice he had finally learned to use even in arguments. "I just can't stand to be told all the time." It was true that one of our workers had a tendency to tire out ears.

"It is quite simple. All you have to do is set yourself to take a shower and clean clothes every other night, and no one need ever tell you." This appeared a wholly new idea to him and he has not since given any offense. Unruly hair still leaves something to be desired, but the first girl will help solve that.

The reading is still a problem. So far as the specialists can find, the vision is normal. When he was sixteen years two months, it was felt that he had himself well enough in hand for an intelligence test. Teachers were amazed at what he knew. He had become an expert listener and fine reader of pictures. The individual Binet was given by a capable examiner. Directions were read to him, and he turned up an I.Q. of 150!

In the house there is a child ten years younger with the same name as Larry's. We three sat near each other a few days after the test.

"Suppose you had gone around here thinking you were no taller than little Larry, and I gave you a yardstick to measure you two, wouldn't you have to change your mind and know you were taller?"

He thought a moment and then said: "No, I don't think so. If I thought I was shorter, just your telling me wouldn't change me."

"Yes, but I didn't *say* it. I gave you a stick to measure."

"Yes, I guess I would have to see it while I was measuring, but next minute I'd forget it, and think as I was small again."

"I was afraid of that. You see the test you took the other day is a yardstick for intelligence. Not entirely accurate but pretty good. Do you know what it said? It said that in native brains you're about thirty points out of a hundred better than I am, and allowing for several times more birthdays I have learned a lot. You can learn anything you want to badly enough."

A few weeks later he ran into the house and said to the only person he found: "Don't you think I'm pretty old not to read?"

The listener agreed, and said that had been the general idea of the trips to the oculist.

When school began next week, he found his teacher of the eighth grade and explained his problem. She offered help if he came early two mornings a week. He did this without fail, although it involved getting his own breakfast those mornings. He mastered the first six readers in as many weeks, but reading is still difficult, the high school teachers are still giving him oral examinations. His long words and scientific terms which he has come on in later years present no difficulty. Words such as which, was, is, with, are still unmastered. They bring on emotional states which blur his vision until he rubs his eyes red. Perhaps these words belong to the years of major emotional upsets and the fear that was present in relation to that terror at home has enveloped all that made up his life at that time. He is left to puzzle out directions on models and under plates in books, but his skill is completely inadequate for those studies which lie between him and his goals. Now, three years after he became the bush expert, most evidences of hostility are gone. He does not hate. He handles criticism without incident. He loves us almost violently, and a few weeks ago when a child who had been rejected from birth by his mother was to come, his help was solicited.

"What's the matter with him?" he asked.

"I'm not sure because I don't know him yet, but I think he thinks people don't like him."

"Not even his folks?"

"Particularly not his folks."

"O.K. I'll do what I can. I should be able to. I ought to know."

He really should and he probably does.

10.

"And what are you taking in college?" a guest was inquiring of Dan who was approaching graduation from college.

"I'm in floriculture, and the army," answered Dan a little whimsically. "I mean, my course is floriculture, but I have also taken R.O.T.C. and will go to camp again this summer, and after that, who knows?"

"You like the work, I presume."

"Oh, yes. I like working with plants and flowers—growing things. If I go back to college when I'm out of the army, however, I might like to move into work with more complicated growing things, children, you know."

"Teaching perhaps. It is in the air here."

"No, I would like to work with children who have special needs —delinquent or unusual ones."

All of us who had been concerned with this college senior since his high school pricked up our ears. Flowers are fine. Skilled growers and arrangers have profitable professions, but this fellow Dan, he was something special. We had watched him grow from a fifteen-year-old who seldom smiled and was subject to black moods which often seemed frighteningly unpredictable. We had seen him grow into a skilled person with children. He was alert to everything, never seemed to act without consideration of his action beforehand. He had rare insight into the difficulties of troubled children, and was able to foresee and deal with futures, so that many difficulties were avoided before they happened at all. He was, in fact, one of those rare people who had learned how to turn all of the liabilities of his own rugged childhood into assets. It had come about in this way.

He was fifteen and school was just out. He had asked permission to swim in the lake. We needed someone to help with the children when they were home all day from school. We went down to watch the swimmers, and one of us to watch this youngster who seemed so promising. We got there just in time to see him quietly put in his place a smart aleck who had reduced one of the small girls to tears by splashing her.

As Dan came out of the water we tackled him, thinking he was the son of a local person unoccupied for the summer vacation. We offered seven dollars a week. His eyes hung out: "They've got a job for me at two dollars a week, but the man isn't quite ready for me. I'd like to come—oh, very much—but I would have to see if the agency would let me."

After a good deal of red tape he was finally transferred to us for the summer to earn his seven dollars and keep. He was a scrupulously neat boy, who always looked, even with the little he had, like a tailor's model. When the end of the first week came and with it the seven dollars, he came and said: "Do you think I could have a dollar to buy a tie?"

"It's your money. You earned it. If you want a tie, of course buy it."

He stood in consternation and said: "You mean you aren't going to keep it for me?"

"Is there any reason for our keeping it? Do you have a wallet? Or a bank account?"

He shook his head and produced from his pocket an old envelope folded up to an inch square from which he produced the seven dollars intact.

"Do you want to save for something special?"

"No, I don't—I mean I'm not used to wanting anything."

"Maybe you would like to buy something special to wear—you could open an account, or if you want we can give you whatever part of your money you want, and we'll pay you at the end of the summer whatever the rest amounts to, all at once."

The free use of two dollars which he decided to take did a great deal toward fostering plans for him. This lack of plan—of wanting anything, which is for most people the early stimulus to work—is so often missing in individuals whose needs are met by impersonal agencies where medical and dental care is a matter of someone driving up and loading up all the clients in the area and packing them off en masse.

The end of that summer came. We had enjoyed Dan and, as always happens, we had acquired an emotional investment in him. There were so many personality problems which marred an otherwise promising person. Again much red tape and by August 15 it was settled that he remain with us and go to school.

We had discovered early that he was ambivalent about us. We sought slow easy ways to make him happy and confident, but this did not seem to touch a curious deep-lying refusal of us. He was deeply appreciative of everything, but held himself in reserve to an alarming extent. One day a young boy whose home life had been disrupted by a badly disturbed mother had expressed his troubled confusion with some marked hostility. All of us were concerned with best measures.

"Why isn't he home with his parents?" Dan blurted out, well-nigh as belligerent as the child under discussion. We were all surprised.

"You know he can't be at home with his mother," someone answered in astonishment.

"Everybody would be all right if they were with their folks. I don't know why you people here take children away from their parents, anyway."

The usually mild mannered boy was aghast at his own explosion, and we were all relieved, for here was the occasion of his withholding from us.

"It is a little different maybe. You see neither we nor anyone else 'takes' these children from their parents. They give them to us and pay us for their care. You needn't feel sorry for them. They like being here and their parents like having them here."

Naturally word explanation could do no more for him than for any of us. We all have to be shown. But explanations sometimes alert one to look for evidence even though they may not change his mind.

As Dan's senior year neared its end, we began to talk about college in a tentative fashion. It was not picked up. "None of my family has ever been to college. Only a few have finished high school." But gradually the talk of schoolmates who were selecting colleges began to waken visions. Catalogs left about, and discussion of the selections made by various of our colleagues' children, abetted a growing interest.

Two scholarships were available. They also helped to make the decision, and so it was that the fall of 1950 saw the boy and his boxes and bedding and whatever arriving on campus.

On the first trip home at Hallowe'en we had visited until fairly late. He was enthusiastically discussing Greek culture as though it were just dug up for the first time. Dan was giving the kind of demonstration of interest in everything which makes an oldster almost willing to grow up again, in order to feel thus violently about any thing.

One of us accompanied him to the door as he started for the residence in which his room lay. He opened the door and started back as though he were physically bumped by the darkness. He realized that it had been seen. He turned and said: "I guess you didn't know I was afraid of the dark."

"Sometimes you startled like this but you always went on, so we just figured you weren't afraid any more."

The facial expression no one can adequately describe and every person experienced with people can recognize crossed his face. Talk was going to be needed, and oldsters have to be ready to receive whenever youth is ready to give.

"I wasn't very big, seven maybe, and I went to the blacksmith shop with the man where we were boarded. It was the first time I heard a man swear! It fascinated me. When I got home I tried it out at the table. The boarding mother made me leave the table and she washed my mouth with soap. That made me throw up, and I was mad."

"Yes, people used to wash children's mouths like that. They thought it was a good way to do," someone said.

Dan continued: "The next day I said it again. It was just before supper. She took me out to the barn and tied me to the cultivator with a rope. She showed me a big rat hole and said that when it got dark the rat would come out and eat me."

There was a hush over the group as we felt the remembered terror spread over us like a fog.

"How long did she leave you there?" someone broke the silence.

Dan hesitated. His fair-mindedness was checking his memory: "Well, not all night I'm sure, but it seemed like it. I used to dream of a rat as big as a wolf about to bite me."

"But now you don't believe in rats or mouth-washing, and you need not remember it any longer."

"How can I forget it?"

"Not exactly forget it, but pull its teeth maybe."

"Did she do it because she wanted to be cruel, do you think?"

"I'm sure she just wanted to be sure I wasn't going to swear any more."

"Did you?"

"Well, yes—but under my breath, I guess."

"So it didn't cure you. It was ignorance and not meanness on her part, so you don't have to remember it against her. If she had known any better, she would have done better, don't you think?"

"But I've been afraid of the dark ever since."

"Getting it off your chest may help that, too. Besides you can't kid any of us about your being afraid. We've watched you go too often."

Dan grinned a little ruefully, and we all went to bed finally, humble about the damage one can do when he is full of good intentions only.

Now Dan would soon be proud possessor of his first degree and maybe, of course, his last as well, but first or last he had grown a useful image of himself. He is one who could go to college even if no other member of his family ever had. From dormitory, he went to a fine fraternity where he has learned a great deal about getting on with people. He had met many less mature, and many with greater natural ability as scholars, but from all he has learned a generous understanding of human frailties and has become more tolerant both of his own and others' weaknesses. Whether his return from service will find him seeking "more complex things to help grow" than plants is anyone's guess. But whether he chooses for his profession the understanding of people or whether he remains with his beloved flowers and understands people as a part of his civic and social obligation, as a sideline, one cannot help but feel a little more confident about the future. He has become a fine person, and he will soon be twenty-two.

11.

"Hi, mom,"—the young voice rang out through the crisp air as Anne climbed out of the car, and strode across the drive and up the steps. My heart swelled with pride. Her uniform of navy blue sat nicely on the square young shoulders. Her eyes were dancing and her head was held high.

The thoughts of all of us went back ten years. What a different arrival that had been, and how unlikely this present triumphant hour seemed then.

To begin where we had cut in so long ago. Anne had been fourteen then. She shuffled rather than walked. Her skin was muddy and basically unclean. Her straight, coarse hair bore tip-end evidence of a strenuous home permanent somewhat earlier. Her lips rolled out to where more mucosa than lip tissue showed. And her eyes—shifty, defiant, hunted, bitter—were somehow pleading and intelligent at the same time.

Attempts at speech revealed spasmodic stuttering which made communication all but unintelligible. Her clothes consisted of a cheap cotton skirt and blouse. She carried a paper sack which contained the rest of her possessions—a woman's slip, large size, instead of a nightgown; a box of bobby pins; and a dirty comb.

The conditions which had brought her an invitation to come were contingent on an older sister who was making a single-handed effort at college, inadequately fed and housed. The sister had come to get fed during the summer and earn a few new clothes against the fall semester. Anne had been at home in dingy poverty with a sixteen-year-old sister, an eighteen-year-old brother, who had been made guardian of the girls, and an invalid brother. The father had disappeared under shadowy conditions somewhat earlier. Next the mother had died. Now tragedy had struck again. The sixteen-year-old had been killed in an accident. If the college girl was to stay on with us the rest of the summer, this child would have to come too. So she had.

"Did you get everything from the car?"

She presented the paper sack, jerking out an agonizing "Yes."

Where to begin?

The sister took her in hand, and soon lunch was served. She ate ravenously, but with some attention to the amenities. Two desserts helped a little. She went about the house peering at one and another thing, watching if she were observed. When the rest of the household went swimming, she expressed no interest, although she walked down to the lake and stood by a few minutes.

When one of us returned to the house an hour later, there was non-stuttering conversation going on. The observer entered quietly to see Anne seated at a table with a small table lamp serving as microphone, while the child acted as master of ceremonies, entertainer, and her own sister, as a member of "the Brown Sisters singing and dancing team." This information came from the announcement she was making of the next act, when she was acting in the emcee role. The selection which she sang was a current sultry blues song, and it carried all the nuances given it by a currently popular radio star.

The observer tiptoed away to report what she had observed. The summer passed quickly. The sister returned to college and we invited Anne to stay on with us. The most characteristic attitude was expressed in the hanging lips, the unsteady eyes, and a quick hostility to any unanticipated question or comment. If anyone could not find a pancake turner, or a mislaid letter, she was quick to volunteer that she did not have it, or was not to blame, or something of the sort.

When she was consulted about what clothes she would like to start school, she was quick to suggest the best and lots of it. When some of us suggested she would need a couple of slips, she spoke up belligerently: "But not any of those cotton ones. I won't put them on." By Labor Day she was modestly outfitted for school with a red flannel topcoat which had been specially made for her and a cocky hat with a quill in it. Shoes presented a problem. A size which could be gotten on she refused for something smaller. Actually her feet were in good proportion to her large frame, but her image of her bodily self was a distorted one, particularly as concerned her head and feet. "Yes, but" was conspicuous in all her speech. In general the yes was a concession, and her real value lay behind the but.

A comfortable second-floor room was freshly papered, curtained, and draped with gay new things. Every morning the light was still blazing in her face. No comment could be secured by question for weeks. Finally it was discovered that she was afraid.

"Afraid of what?"

"Tramps might get in the house and come up the stairs to get me."

It was pointed out that there were no tramps for miles, and then none who might enter houses. "But snakes might come up from outside and get in the windows." The complete inanity of the substances of her fears might have led us to doubt the quality of her intelligence except that fears would probably be less numerous for all of us if they were accessible to reason.

The first two years showed so little progress as to leave us often discouraged. At home she was critical and often uncooperative. She seemed interested in getting herself into messes with members of the household, and continued each with mounting tensions until a swearing, weeping tirade left her exhausted and threw her back upon a recital of her woes until she had wept herself into someone's good graces.

When first she caught the idea of friendliness she began putting it to the test. When a school acquaintance tried to be friendly she would accept the advances and then play some practical joke which was calculated to rebuff the person. Then the friend would become incensed. Anne would retell the incident and finish by saying: "You see, I'm right, no one does like me."

Years passed with slow progress. She finished high school and was helped to business college. It was her choice, yet she attended irregularly. She was often tardy. Finally she was given an ultimatum which was carried through. At the end of the second year she was ready to take a job. She lived with us. Her training went on both at home and on the job. Eventually she seemed ready to leave and took a position in a nearby city. Her experience in boarding houses and on a job where none knew her began a rapidly maturing period. Now finally success attended a problem worked on from the beginning. To make that clear we must return to her childhood.

After the father's disappearance, the distraught mother often took the small baby and Anne, who was four, to religious meetings at river-front missions, where drunks were converted in the winter and became backsliders in the spring sunshine. Anne had made grotesque sense out of the exhorting and shouting and vivid picturings of hell and damnation. She herself had picked up a picturesque line of profanity on the streets which were her playground. The mother who was an essentially fine person undertook to punish her out of it. Mouth-washing plus the threats of hell had given Anne a curiously potent depressive understanding. Those who confessed their sins and promised to sin no more were uniquely damned if they did not keep their promises. She had frequently pledged herself to the Eternal that she would never "take his name in vain" again, and as often as rage and resentment overtook her, so often did she regress to her colorful language.

This practice she believed had already and irrevocably damned her and hell was a certainty when she died. Logically enough then she was preoccupied in avoiding death, and tramps up the front stairs and snakes up the back walls, drowning in the swimming pool, wasps, worms—everything indeed—took on the flavor of the fear of death, not for death, but for the inevitable burning which blazed behind it.

All our specific attempts to free her from her fears were blind stabs in the dark, in that first year. In the second and subsequent ones we began to see that some over-all constellation of fear was at work. She lacked insight herself and we lacked the wit to find her trouble.

Finally, in what began as a casual conversation about some fear expressed, one of us inquired: "Can't you think of any special scare you had when you were little?" Her eyes opened big to the outside and wider, apparently, inside. Then came a specific story of a teary and beery return to virtue after repeated returns to vice on the part of an old reprobate in the mission. All the details came out. He had said he was lost forever, and apparently the exhorter agreed with him.

On such an agglutinized mass of terrors and frights the child had come by these fixations of damnation. Years passed in which the girl studied comparative religions, talked with priests, rabbis, and ministers, and worked herself clear from the maze of religion-inspired terrors. Six years after this clearance began, it somehow found a completion. Her answer was not selected from any of the readymade ones she encountered. None of the philosophies or religions which any of us lived by satisfied her. She tailored her own to fit her own needs.

She began to be free of obscure physical difficulties which had been thought functional. She began to make advancement in her professional work. The Naval Reserve loomed as a possible answer to a compelling purpose which she had had to suppress when learning to swim held its threat of death. With the water no more dangerous to her than to any other person, she also mastered that.

The last barrier to be burned away was the stuttering. As her desire to communicate became genuine, she was able to throw her bridges from herself to others with increasing skill.

Now she had come home after a four-year stretch in Naval Reserve, and her eager young voice, her firm footfall, her outstretched young arms were a sight indeed.

"Hi mom," she had called. "It's so good to be home." Much, much later when the plans for her sister's wedding were discussed, and all her vivid experiences retold, I asked, "And what is next on your agenda?"

"I'm going to re-enlist for two years. I can go in the regular navy now. I'm going to look like heck for the right man. If I don't find him, I'll re-enlist for twenty years. Then I can retire on pay, and with my savings I'm going to start a nursery. I shall employ only those who love children and have fun the rest of my life."

CHAPTER VI

How Shall We Educate?

In the totalitarian regime, it is the function of the teacher to be the counterpart of the drill sergeant in the army. . . . He tells them what to think; he drills them in blind obedience to orders. In sharp contrast, the teacher in a democracy is, or at least ought to be, truly an educator, helping his students learn how to think for themselves, drawing out their latent capacities, permitting them to develop so that they will grow and hopefully flower, each in his own best way. Between telling students what to think and helping them to learn how to think, there is a chasm as wide and deep as the Grand Canyon of the Colorado River.

—KIRTLEY MATHER

1.

Behind the behavior of each of us lie the beliefs upon which we predicate our action. For teachers these beliefs are more crucial than for many other professions, since they affect the actions of a host of oncoming persons as well as guiding the behavior of the teacher as an individual. But these beliefs do not stay fixed any more than do other products of growth. New experiences may yield both additive and corrective values. Yet most people find changes in these areas of belief difficult. A changed belief may call for a changed action, not only just now but from now on. This is a more fear-provoking thing to contemplate than merely behaving differently this time. To change one's mind and follow this change with consistently and persistently changed action is usually a test of one's courage.

We have undertaken to do a difficult thing in this volume. We have tried to describe the process by which we came to our beliefs or assumptions, rather than simply relating the new beliefs which the process built. We have gone one step further. We have described also the process within which we undertook to change our ways to a closer matching with our changed beliefs. Finally, we have undertaken to describe processes of growth which we observed with different children over prolonged periods of time. These descriptions are a manner of word movie from which the observer draws what inferences his yesterdays permit.

Now we are undertaking to show what we feel are implications for public education. We do not state these as generalizations but describe them in action. For this purpose we took our built-in movie camera into many schools and school rooms, where some administrator or individual teacher had undertaken to give substance and action to beliefs similar to those we profess. We have seen them one place and another over the nation's school system. They are factual to this extent. They have all been observed. They are fictional to the extent that we have compressed them in time, to meet the exigencies of the printed page. They are here delineated as living concretions of what would otherwise have to be static and lifeless generalizations.

2.

"Not a new vintage building, is it?" one said to the other, as we walked up to the front door of a twenty-year-old school building. Once inside, age was modified by the bright paint, tile floor, and absence of that tangible odor, if not of sanctity, at least of long occupation by humanity, which characterizes so many school buildings.

The principal, herself a mother, greeted us warmly and inquired what we wished to see. "We are interested in watching some work with children about fourth-grade level," we replied.

"I can't do exactly that," she replied, "because we do not use that type of grouping here." This we had known, and since we wanted to find some evidence of the working out of the concept of ongoingness, we had chosen this school, known for some years in a wide circle of educators for its abandonment of the conventional grade organization of one through eight.

"These children are one of six such groups in this building where the major number of the children have been attending school three years—and this far into the fourth year since leaving kindergarten. There are included also a few—three I think—who have been in school two years and this much of a third year since kindergarten. The rest maybe six or seven, had been in school four years before the beginning of this semester."

"So they differ in chronological age?"

"Yes, but it is not more wide than in any other method of grouping. Look for yourself," she continued, as she opened a door into a bright room, at the moment empty in the middle of the floor. From behind the piano one and then another curious head rose at the sound of the closing door. They looked us over and returned to a mass of strings in a tangle. Puppets had been put by too carelessly, or two children had undertaken to handle them at the same time. Six or seven were injecting advice and fingers. In the far corner eight or ten children sat in a semicircle. They appeared to have books all alike. One was reading aloud. Midway of the wall diminutive furniture included two plastic-covered rocking chairs. A boy in one and a girl in the other were rocking in rhythm, which was achieved by grasping each other's nearest hands. Both had different books in their other hands, rocking and reading in complete isolation, in the midst of thirty children all otherwise occupied. So far no teacher had been in sight. Now two children at the edge of a huddle at the board came to us. "I'm Jane and this is Billy. Do you want us to show you our room?" We did. The tour began.

"We won't go too close to that group," Jane said, pointing to several children grouped around three tables pushed into one.

"Why?" we inquired.

"They are awful busy, getting everything planned for the puppet show. We have invited Miss Shaw's room for next Friday. We want everything just right. Those children haven't been in school as long as we have. We want the words of the speeches not too hard."

"This," volunteered Billy, "is kind of messy. We won't do this again. I guess you can see on this map, where we pulled off the Indians. That's what we made the map for. It took a lot of us a long time. We hated to throw it away. Some of us thought we could use it for our western study. Those are products we are putting on, but the shadows, like, of the Indians show through."

"You are studying products beginning here in Michigan, are you?"

"Well, yes," Jane answered somewhat puzzled. "Do you mean, why didn't we begin on the Atlantic coast? Of course we could. But, well, this is where we are and besides we all like Roy Rogers, and we thought we would start from where we are and go where he is. Cowboys, Indians, and covered wagon people are more interesting I think than pilgrims and coal miners. We'll do them another time," she concluded.

Now the teacher who had been on a small chair at the center of the huddle rose to greet us.

"We were so busy over here I didn't hear you come in. The people here are getting a puppet show ready for guests next week. An Indian medicine man sings and dances in this play. The children got the text of his song from some searching in the library. It was translated into prose. They think it must be rhymed poetry, so that's what we were doing. I'm not much good to them. I'm surely no poet."

Some loud talk was coming from the board of directors' table. "I tell you we daresn't have a rattlesnake. It would scare those little kids."

"And besides who ever heard of a puppet snake? Where would you put the string on his rattles?"

The teacher moved over to the table.

"Let me in on the question."

Everyone tried to oblige.

"I can't hear you all. You will break our guests' eardrums. Please one of you tell our guests and me—by the way this is Dr. Rasey and Dr. Menge from Wayne University, come to visit our school."

This pause for amenities had given the change of focus to bring their problem out of the feeling into the reasoning stage. It was settled unanimously to put a clay snake on the stage beside the cactus, borrowed, as they told us, from the office for the play—"not ours for keeps."

A mother with a bulgy knitting bag had just come in. The children had the puppets untangled. The readers were still reading and rocking.

"Good morning, Mrs. Johns, it is wonderful you can come, just today when we're so busy."

"Where shall we go?" the mother asked.

"The second-floor library nook will be large enough. You people who are learning to knit—Mrs. Johns is here. Will you take her up to the library corner?"

Children detached themselves from various groups; each had produced a ball of gay cord and knitting needles from the cupboard.

"Are you the art teacher, Mrs. Johns?" we inquired.

"Oh no," she laughed. "I'm a room mother here who volunteers to take care of a few children when there is need. No, I'm no teacher—just a mother who can teach knitting, that's all."

We thought that the word "just" didn't belong in the sentence, as she moved off with her brood of ten or twelve like a female pied piper.

"Is this—usual?" we asked.

"Goodness, yes. With all these children are doing, one teacher couldn't keep track of it all, let alone do it. I forgot she was coming today, but it will make it easier for these children over here to practice with the puppets. You see, these are what in the old days we called slow readers. They read and read, to get their part learned."

"You don't use your best readers for actors then?"

The teacher looked puzzled and said, "No, I know what you mean—no, we try to help those who don't read well to get to be better readers. No sense to this repetitive practice for the ones who already read well."

"You like this arrangement of no grades, do you?" we inquired.

"Yes, I like it very much. At first there seems to be more work, but actually you have more time to yourself for the special needs. We are trying to live with the fact that all the children are growing, but each at his own rate. That fellow over there is just beginning to perk. He's average, or maybe a little better, but not much. He's just a slow grower. That girl over there is a year older than anyone else. She came from a remote rural area and didn't start school until she was eight. The change to urban environment was difficult for the family, but she is coming fine. She will be ready for junior high school in two years, I'm sure."

"What do you judge readiness by?"

"We give standarized tests twice a year in the basic areas. We usually preface then by a day of measuring height and weight. We discuss differences in these items, and introduce the tests as more yardsticks and scales. There is a minimum of tension. The children put themselves under best conditions, just as they "stand tall against the door-casing to be measured.""

"And the principal is armed with evidence for those who think children can't learn if they enjoy what they are doing," said the principal who had returned for us.

"That problem, here too?"

"Yes but it grows less and less. The evidence has been piling up for several years now. Some parents find it difficult to see when their children first come to this school."

"You were asking me if I liked it," the teacher picked up again. "I want to say that it solves so many problems. No promotions makes report card grades unnecessary. In the whole ongoingness of each child we can mind what is best for him—real respect for the individual."

"It is even more than that, I think. It is this day in this child's life. It's his life in his epoch, reaching back to his parents and ahead to his children, on and on," one of us said.

"And that gives real meaning to what I'm doing. I'm not scared of my job or even discouraged very much or often. This puppet show is, of course, not cosmic. If it falls flat it won't wreck either me or the children, but if it succeeds, then there is no break in the lifeline."

We thought that a strong pulsing of life was in evidence here.

We were made comfortable in the office and presently were served trays with a fine lunch by three girls who said with pride that they were receptionists. "We look after guests," they said, "and we have lots of them."

"How do you get to be receptionists?" we inquired. "Does your teacher select you?"

Again that puzzled look, and then one of comprehension. "No— well yes. We are all in our last year here. We can't have our chance until then. We volunteer when the chance comes, but the teacher does help us learn how to ask strangers their names, and introduce them, and at meal time ask . . . Oh dear, I brought you both coffee without asking what do you prefer?"

We responded that we both were coffee drinkers.

"Then when our teacher thinks we are ready, we go alpha- betically and take our turns."

Left alone with the principal we both began to question at once. "What about discipline? Do patrons approve? Are the children all as wonderful as we see?"

It had been three years since any teacher had sent a pupil to the principal for discipline. She did not think it would occur ever, unless some new child coming in found the novelty too trying. Yes, the patrons approved in general, especially since the test returns showed—as one father put it—all that the old driving methods produced, plus human relations skills, plus a habit of happiness. We pondered that one—"a habit of happi- ness."

Finally as we rose to go, the principal said, "I'm happy you liked our school, and that you found concrete examples of your theories. I'm going to take over 'ongoingness' as a term. 'Growth,' which we have been using, is too narrow, too hindering, and your discussion of it makes me feel a fresh dignity to our job as co- creators in an ever new, ever changing world."

3.

"You might enjoy seeing our rhythm class," the principal of the private school was saying as we moved through the corridors to the gymnasium. The young man in charge was sitting in loose informal clothes and barefoot, in the middle of the floor, with an oversize tom-tom between his knees. He teaches dance at a nearby college. We arrived by one door as the children trooped in by another. There were two children under three; ten or twelve were six to eight, including one large eight-year-old girl, over- weight, squarely built, with a dozen signs which would have led us at Rayswift to put her into the hands of an endocrinologist at once.

The long hand of the teacher tapped lightly, a simple rhythm on the tom-tom. The children also barefoot sat round about him. A student teacher rode herd on the two little ones when their exploration took them too far afield. Simple suggestions, with a querying up-voice, led children from swimmers on the polished floor to crabs on the sand, elephants, rabbits, and the like.

The drumstick which the young man had with him was not used for drumming but served once at least as a hurdle for the children to leap over when they were prancing horses. We were at once impressed with the fact that no second trials were suggested for those who did not succeed. No change of posture or facial expression gave the slightest indication of distinction between "coulds" and "could nots."

As the period progressed, the rhythms became far more complicated and the movements became more intricate too. The fat child responded with as much abandonment of self as any other, and the stocky, clumsy, awkward-looking body appeared to be floating above the surface of the floor. We watched this with astonishment. Generally this child, we thought, would have found difficulty joining with a group on a floor at all. We might have expected her to have an image of her physical self which would have precluded this giving of herself to movement.

As we continued to look we saw that the everybody-is-doing-what-he-can attitude had its corollary, whatever-he-can-is-good-enough. It became plain that this handicapped child had, through her two years' stay here, built for herself such a sense of "I can" that she could say "yes" to herself with the inevitable result of grace and ease. We thought it inevitable, since the flow of human movement where no basic illness is involved is, by the nature of the pulsing of energy, rhythmic and smooth. It becomes, apparently, less than that only when a consciousness of can'tness rises into the image and by that interference breaks the rhythm and the smooth becomes jerky. The session came to a close with the invitation to "do what you feel the music tells you."

As we spoke with the teacher later he said: "Yes, I do that way with my pupils for several reasons. In the first place, a child handles himself as well as he can. If he could do better, he would —and as he can, he will. If I take each child's performance for just that, I will put no ideas into his head that he can't or didn't succeed, or is clumsy and all such hindering things."

"Why do you think such things hinder? Doesn't he find out finally that he doesn't and can't?"

He paused a moment, and then said: "I think it is best for everyone to have a picture of himself succeeding, or at least not failing. If we think we fail, well, we can't quite try. And for your second question, I want to say yes and no. Of course he finds out that he doesn't—that's the yes; but he doesn't get the idea he can't. It's just he doesn't. And it is he who finds out he doesn't. I don't intensify the picture he has of not doing with my pronouncement that he can't. Anyway I have no crystal ball. How do I know he can't? All I can know is that he doesn't, and I don't need to shout about that."

"Would you say," we continued, "that what you do by no correction is to offer the child a more positive image of himself as one who can, whether he is one who does or not, at the moment?"

"Yes, I'd buy that," was his rejoinder.

In another school we saw a teacher doing a similar thing in a ninth-grade English class. The group had read the Perfect Tribute, out of some concern about Lincoln's Gettysburg Address in a social studies class. They had enriched themselves greatly with the emotional picture there presented, and had returned again and again to the speech itself, finding new meaning as they went. It happened that they had begun the semester with this project, which expanded itself since a boy newly come from Illinois marveled that February 12 was not a school holiday in Michigan.

"We should celebrate some way," one of them had said.

"Party?"

"Not that—birthday party for someone dead?" General laughter followed this adolescent humor.

Finally they decided to learn the speech and select one of their number who did it well to present it for both their room and their neighbors'.

A big fellow said he was willing to try to say it about ten minutes after he had begun to study. He was always over-estimating himself. He was invited to begin. He rose and faced his classmates. The unfamiliar four score and ten threw him. Everyone laughed at his discomfiture. He offered to lick them all and sundry, one after the other. It was pointed out by a classmate that even if he could, what would that prove?

"It's all right for you fellows to laugh," the teacher was saying. "It's not too easy to do that. If James made a mistake thinking he was ready too soon, you, likely enough, will make that same mistake yourself, or even the opposite of not getting ready until the date is passed."

We cite this incident because it is of a piece with the hundreds of similar circumstances every teacher meets every day. A near failure left interpreted only by the derisive laughter of those who can't do as well can be one more grain of grit to scar the gears of general doing. When young people have faith in their ability, and that is most often the case, the small sour flavor of near failure can be utilized in the total experience, if it does not sour the experience. The teacher's opinion verbalized serves as a mirror serves to give back one's face. Although it is only a reflection—and that is as close to seeing our own faces as we will ever come—it gives back the verdict of a judge one trusts, and her emphasis on the positive leaves the erstwhile failure free to grow to success.

As we came through the grounds in the same campus, a small boy caught up with us and inquired our names. We returned the courtesy, but he was so slow in answering that we both looked down at once to see if he had heard us. It was plain that he was studying his response. "I suppose," said he, "that I am the best adder in the second grade." When we told this to one of our thin-lipped colleagues, she answered, "When he gets to the third grade, he'll find more than addition." We hoped he would not find her or her kind when he did get to the third grade, but even if he did, he was securer in his own image of himself from his own evaluation, and will be the better able to withstand the on-slaughts of such as find their satisfaction entirely in what they know which little children do not yet know.

In still another school we saw an English teacher handing back themes. The eager eyes and outstretched hands gave evidence that the pupils were *eager* to receive their papers after the teacher had had them. This called for investigation. As she walked about she was dropping small comments. "I must say I enjoyed every one of these papers. What an idea you have here, Harry. You know what it made me think of? I always wanted to sew when I was a young girl. I sewed so fast that I didn't sew well. My mother used to say that I sewed with a burned thread and a red-hot needle. I got so mad trying to find out what actually you were saying with your henscratch writing—and such an exciting idea, too."

Once, she paused before a big, awkward, overgrown youth and said: "Did you imagine that fishing episode, or had you heard or read it somewhere? I hope it was yours, because it was wonderful." The big fellow answered: "I fixed a little better from what my granddad told me happened to him."

Then the teacher turned to the board and wrote eight words, trick words which have made all of us trouble one time or another. As she turned back, she said: "I don't remember who had trouble with which. It doesn't matter if you will all notice." Then briefly she pointed out the snare in each of the words—"against the next time you want to use them."

When we asked to see one of the pupil's papers we discovered the error, but there was no check above it, red or blue underlining, or frame to point out to the offender the wrong way and make it difficult to correct it. Instead, in the margin she had, without comment, written the word correctly.

"Don't you ever indicate misspelled words?" we asked.

"No—I like this way better. Sometimes when we have a few minutes to spare I say, to this class particularly: "Last week I found twelve misspelled words in your papers. Would you like to see if you can spell them now? Then we do write them like an old-fashioned spelling lesson. I spell them correctly on the board. They check their own papers, and keep their own scores."

"Isn't that unusual?"

"I don't know about that. It isn't for us. The way I have it figured is that those who want to spell correctly have the chance to learn. Those who haven't had success enough with their writing to care yet will not profit by my finding fault with them."

"You said, 'particularly this class.' Do you find twelve words a lot for this grade?"

"No—this class has a good many children with poor visual memory—poor spellers. Twelve words as the assignment doesn't come from the number they misspelled. Twelve words are what I figure they can learn. I select those words from those usually learned in this grade. After all, twelve a week gets to be a lot of words, and mostly they do learn that many each week."

"Would you say that the child who sees himself as one who spells well is likely to be more spelling-learning-minded than one who sees himself as one who can't spell?"

"Naturally," she responded, and we thought she may have spoken more accurately than she knew.

Speaking with an eminent psychiatrist, we said: "What do you hold about the image of the self?"

He hesitated a moment and then said: "Different people of course see these things differently. Some even name them differently. They say self-perception, self-image, image of the self, ego damage, and on and on. If, however, we look a little below terminology there is general agreement. What was the song? 'Accentuate the positive?' Well, that's not just a song. It is an attitude deriving from research and creative thinking in many areas of human affairs.

"Since we have come to know the mechanics of human energy expenditure we see that the once glorified human will is not so potent, in fact is helpless, unless it is accompanied by the older, more potent drive of desire, of want-to-ness. It is a pity that these two concepts have such unfortunate second meanings. The term 'desire' is often only a label for sex drives or food or drink or drug hunger, a negative connotation, particularly in our culture, descended as it is in some sections from the grayest and most barren concepts of coldness, grimness, and repression of all that is pleasurable.

" 'Want to' has suffered from its association with the adverb just. When people say 'just as they want to,' it has the flavor of whim, passing fancy, or a kind of pure cussedness. Actually it takes an endocrine product to release the stored sugar, which fuels the muscles, which in turn do the behaving for all of us. I never expect much improvement in a patient unless and until he wants to get well. They often come somewhat daring a doctor to help them. Until that barrier is removed he can't, either."

We thought that this point of view coincided with our own, but we asked, "Now in our field a teacher often says that a child *wouldn't* do something like learn spelling words, but she *made* him. If we understand you correctly she not only did not make him, she can't make him. Are we right?"

"I think so, certainly. What actually the teacher does, and all she does here, is to remove his purposes and desires still further from spelling. He argues with himself, it will be the quickest way to get rid of her, who hinders me from going swimming, keeping me here spelling. So I'll make like I have changed my mind, and get to swimming quicker. So he does. Measured a few days later he is found to have increased his rate of forgetting to match his enforced increase in spelling. So what you have here is a revolutionary, destroying the project of spelling by wanting no part of it, and as here, sabotaging its small gains.

"No, I would surely say that compulsion is wasted effort, and like most energy on the loose, does damage—damage to the attitude, purposes, the skills of the enforced learner, and damage to the disposition, arteries, blood pressure, and digestion of the enforcer."

"Would you say that the image of self of a healthy learner, as well as of your sick patients, is crucial to his doing?"

"Exactly. Crucial because of mechanical reasons. If he thinks he can't, he can't as long as he thinks so. Hard, but true. If your pupil believes himself one who can learn if he wants to, and moreover can want to, when he wants something else, too, and at the same time, you have not only one who will learn now but one who will be able to 'change and keep on changing as long as he lives.' For my money, it's all the years after school, as well as the years in school. Suppose you could scare him into studying, are you going to follow him 'all the days of his life,' breathing down his neck?"

4.

"How do you know," a colleague was saying, as a few of us of different educational faiths were lunching together, "How do you know that your student ever sweats, if he has to be helped to a good picture of himself before he can do anything?"

"In the first place the term 'work' has different meanings when we say he works on the highway, or is working a puzzle. In the first case there are sweat glands pretty evenly distributed over the surface of the body to help throw off the waste material incident to effort expended through the muscles. In the second case—and my students are not working muscularly in my class—the work is done by various processes associated with mentation. Muscles are almost at rest—barring eye, mouth, or finger muscles, turning pages or writing. There are no sweat glands involved. The tasks are dissimilar. The same figures do not hold."

"No, no that isn't fair. He doesn't mean sweat drops—although you are right. It is an inapt figure. I know of course. What I think is often ignored in this area of thinking is that the term 'individual' is just that—that which can be no further divided. The person has an integrity—an integerness, a oneness—which is inviolable. We never make anyone do anything. He makes himself, or he gives consent if under duress. We knew early, and many peoples are finding later, that slave labor—that done under the purposes of another and unshared—does not produce kind or quantity of product as does free men's labor, whether on production lines, rice fields, or school desks.

"In the last analysis what we do comes from us; what we know, which makes us do, comes from us; and what we know and do *is* us."

"Suppose that in my pupil there is nothing known and nothing done, then what?"

"Actually this state cannot exist. The newborn knows, briefly, how to suck. When he doesn't use it, like any skill, he loses it. Before that, tissues knew how to formulate themselves, always from less to more, from simpler to more complex, from the first searching sperm and ovum, who had what they knew, from before time when there had been other gleams in other papa's eyes. Living tissue is purposive and has its knowing to trigger it."

"Now you are going metaphysical on us."

"I confess that I would have been not long ago, when metaphysics meant things we knew too little about to discuss, and which lay outside the realm of established fact. But these items are not a matter of conjecture any more. Things are always moving from the unknown to the known. So I deny the allegation. I speak of known demonstrable evidence. The meaning of what we see comes from us. We make our knowledge as we go, by making it our own. We build ourselves out of ourselves and later out of each other. We can not do things *to* people, but only with them. Every man is uniquely alone and king in his own domain, but driven, if he wants more or better, to make friends with his neighboring kings and kingdoms, and share and be shared."

"Suppose you had a group of overgrown boys in eighth-grade grammar. They don't want any part of it. They are waiting for releasing birthdays. Now, what does your science make of that?"

"In the first place I should try not to get caught in this unscientific spot. For twenty-five years we have had evidence that learning the rules of grammar does not improve language usage. If, however, I was pushed into this spot, we would not crack a book until we had exhausted conversation among us about whatever the boys were interested in."

"They aren't interested in anything."

"Finish your sentence."

"I did."

"I'm sorry, you didn't. Isn't it, 'in anything I know about or appreciate'?"

"Well, yes."

"Then find another word. Interested means *inter*—that midst in which *esse*—I have my being. Your boys—I won't make a long guess—are having their being in the midst of duels, souped-up cars, airplane gas, pistons, and queer as it may sound to you, a stranger in this paradise, they are saying things to each other. If you don't know the language, it is easy to learn. Incidentally do you know a good English term for 'souped up'? You don't, nor anyone else, any more than we could use resiliency when we mean pep.

"Once we have something to talk about amongst ourselves,

we can start talking. We speak with or against grammar principle. But correct speech is a muscular skill learned by doing, and without benefit of much generalization upon the anatomy of language. Now, if finally you are so stubborn that you just have to have your own way, you may lead them into a concern about the workings of verbs—they are elements of action—as they have been interested in pistons.

"They can easily be induced to give themselves to an understanding of the functioning parts of a sentence; but if your information is correct and they are waiting a releasing birthday, the bones of the language they will seldom write may be of less value than a skillful wielding of the words they know. Do you remember the junior who three times failed freshman English, and was finally asked to leave, since manifestly he had no skill in language? Remember that before the term was over he had sold his professor a set of books he didn't want, couldn't use, and couldn't afford, with what must have been pretty effective language."

"So what you are saying is that the teacher doesn't have a chance to do anything for a pupil, unless the pupil gives his consent."

"No and yes. No to the first. A teacher has all the chance there is to help people *with* their growing—but no chance to do things *to* people. When one tries to help people it has to be done *with* people. Maybe that is a process *evolved*—a manner of selection and adaptation on the human level. Maybe it was *involved*—in man by divine fiat. The fact remains that a person does select, and only *he* can move his muscles to do or to say. So I must say 'yes' to the second part of your statement. Medical people have pointed out the ineffectiveness of their medicines where there was no desire to live. It's hard but it's true. Move up circumstance so close he has to fall over it. Prod and encourage. Help create a positive image of self. It's the same horse at the tank. He has to do the drinking. So does the learner."

"Yes, I see your point—but it is tedious waiting, and nerve-racking."

"Now we are in complete argreement for once! Learners must

often be waited for. It is often tedious for the waiter. If you have nerves, I suppose they'll be worn raw unless you can come to know that the learner isn't being slow just to annoy you. When we can remember that our responsibility ends with having arrayed the table with the best we know, as easily accessible as we know, and inviting the guest to eat, the odds are with life then and we can do no more. We need not be irritated that our best has not been good enough—yet."

5.

The meeting had been adjourned. We had been members of a panel, discussing with parents and teachers, "What of education—past, present, future?" The usual group surrounded a few panel members to raise questions or state convictions, largely about present practices.

"I don't get it," the manifestly successful young businessman was saying. "Why all this fuss about socialization, getting along with people? Why so much school time put in on such things? My kids get on with people too well. We have the whole neighborhood in the playroom. What do they need to learn about that?"

We looked at each other. One of us said: "That is another word like 'want to' that has more than a surface meaning. Have you ever had an employee who rubbed you the wrong way? What did you do about him?"

"Fired him of course."

"Did he do his work well?"

"Well, yes, he did—maybe too well—but he could get more folks mad faster than anyone I ever saw."

"Then you understand perfectly what we are talking about. It is not just a question of being a good host, or the life of the party, although these are useful skills."

"You see," the other added, "when we say 'get on with people,' we mean a lot more basic thing. We mean that all get farther along—not just one over the tops of others."

"And to do that, we have to be able to see and hear other people as a first step."

"What do you mean?"

"I have been in meetings where no one listened because they were each trying to get a chance to say what they wanted. One has to listen creatively as well as critically. He has to see who is speaking, not by name, but by nature. If it is one embittered by what he thinks are raw deals for him, he will not be able to hear you until this has been drained off. If you feel you are right you can afford to wait and listen."

"Then what? Most meetings I go to end up in a squabble and the few persistent ones have their way."

"If that is true, as you see it, then it is just evidence of how much they need precisely the training we are talking about. But I think you are quite right to say: 'What next?' Next comes the careful planning, the fusing of the points of view of others, and a final single plan which all can give themselves to. Then there are all the things that can befall a good plan when immature people get to quarreling over who and what are most important."

"And let's not forget the actual carrying out, and passing judgments on the job."

"But—it didn't used to be like that. It was every man for himself."

"Yes, that was before assembly lines, division of labor, and our recent ways of life. My grandmother could rock and knit stockings for the lot of us. Or get a meal from the rooster walking in the barnyard to the pumpkin in its shell. Now it takes an army of workers to make a stocking, and no one of them can do it alone."

"Yes, for better or worse we're sold to mass production."

"And in almost any area you can name, it calls for togetherness, team work, interpersonal relations; labor and management; international and national problems. It is no longer only a good religious practice or good philosophy to love your neighbor as yourself. Learning to get on together is a survival tool, like language and the three R's and the like. Now we need a new tool for new problems."

The arguing speakers and the hangers-on nodded their agreement.

"You know, I think you have made a convert, but I want to think some more about it."

"But you see, we aren't in the convert-making business. We are in the relating business. You said, 'what about this?' and we said, 'yes, but have you looked at this?' We looked with you. You looked with us, and we all saw more than we did before. Now what each of us makes of what we saw is his own responsibility."

With his hat in his hand and half way to his head, the gentleman said: "Well, for the love of Pete—that's what my son's high school teacher must have meant. He came home from freshman English and said the teacher had told them she would make them as uncomfortable as she could until they began to think. It was not her job to tell them *what* to think, but very much her job that they *thought something*. By George, yesterday I thought that was nonsense."

SUMMING UP

Samuel Crothers once said of Boston that it is not so much a place as a state of mind. Rayswift, we think, is not only a state of mind but a state of being as well. To have been a part of this state of mind and being with children—there have been fifty-four in all—is to have learned widely and deeply from them. The children have been our teachers as we watched their behavior, were party to their decision-making, and began to understand the values which released the selves they are into purposive action. We have learned from them much about action and the springs of action. They have taught us much about ourselves, and about adult relationships with children as, mirror-like, they have reflected us to ourselves.

Some of the things we have learned are concrete and specific enough to summarize in an attempt to communicate our findings. These learnings have largely to do with methods of study and principles of nurture. We believe these matters can be useful to all teachers, and to those who stand in a teacher-type relation to children. Some of our conclusions should be of special usefulness to teachers and parents who must meet the needs of superior children in the midst of less able children in family group or in classrooms.

Four generalizations are presented here in the form of suggested procedures. We have incorporated them into our own practices and are prepared to recommend them to other teachers engaged in studying and nurturing the learning of children or adults.

1. *In studying the development of a person look for the whole pattern of movement of the "energy→purpose→achievement" dynamic.* A personality can be comprehended only when approached as a totality. A comprehension of the whole self cannot be synthesized from any amount of discrete data. "Assembling" from these data cannot "add up," since actually the personality is more product than sum. The meaning of the whole coherence is to be discovered only in the interrelatednessses of its parts. One is what he does. What he does is an ongoingness set up by the energy he is or the energy which has passed over lines of purpose toward consummation.

Our first question with a new child is concerned with his "doingness." Toward what is his energy directed? Is it achieving his purposes? If it appears to fail in this we can begin to investigate where, in the process, the failure lies. If there is little or no achievement—the easiest place to see—we may investigate the purposive sequence. Is it inadequate in its formulation? Is it inadequate in its function? If these do not yield the answer, we are ready to investigate whether or not there is energy available to fuel a purpose.

Once these investigations begin they will employ the same methods and bring up the same type of data as the cumulative records in common use. Blood count, wrist and digital X-ray, basal metabolism, blood sugar, as well as height-weight records (interpreted on grids), family histories, and the rest. The difference lies in the fact that these investigations are never considered apart from the total integrated pattern of energy expenditure.

The fruitfulness of the "total" approach is documented repeatedly in our records. Heidi, it will be recalled, had a history of nonachievement, bone X-rays with a history of malnutrition, severe emotional shocks. She initiated few purposes of her own and held aloof from those of others. She was suspected of low mentality, and gave evidence of such when examined by those who failed to take the total equation into account. When examiners knew how to release her to herself she gave evidence of a little better than average intelligence. Yet she showed a quick mastery of a new language, fair ability to read and handle the simple mathematics required of her age group. She did well in first grade, and overzealous parents took her progress thus far for cure. She was taken away from her usual companions to a new school, to a new house in a new section of her city; and to complete the picture, she was given a new first and last name. The old pattern reasserted itself, and what might have been will not be.

Leslie taught us the same thing. He came to us with a mass of records from some of the nation's best experts. All the "facts" were in those records. Conditions of birth were normal. It was eight days later when he aspirated an entire bottle of milk and spent weeks in an oxygen tent with a feeding tube. That was recorded by someone else in another place. Difficulty in swallowing was observed in still another place. His annual growth in height in his seventh year and his eighth was one-tenth of an inch.

When we observed his total doingness, it was seen that he didn't swallow what he chewed, but bided his time to be rid of the bulk in his mouth. "He doesn't swallow" revealed, as it was pursued to the source, meaning and results. Glandular tests showed a low pituitary. Medication and re-education of the total personality resulted in the ninth-year growth of 2.1 inches, and the tenth year not yet completed is so far a bit above normal. He will not be a dwarf.

We are convinced that the way to observe a child is always to see him whole. No matter what unique or seemingly bizarre elements show up in the data, we are careful to maintain the integrity of the original equation, with each new finding being introduced into it as the relationships among factors become clear.

2. *Arrange circumstances which surround the learner in such a way that it is easy rather than hard for him to learn—the organism must do its own growing and learning.* As corollary, be pleased with your role as scene shifter and stage manager. In a sense we do not teach a child language, reading, mathe-

matics, or anything else. The most we can do, and all that needs doing, is to set the stage in such a fashion that it is as easy, or pleasant, or profitable for the learner to learn as it can be made. We lead him to water. He drinks or doesn't. No one can drink for him.

We cannot feed an anemic child. He must feed himself. We cannot uncripple a spastic child. We can provide the one with food and attitudes toward it. And the other, as happened in one case of severe spasticity at Rayswift, we could provide with play materials with which he improved his handling of himself from semi-helplessness to adequacy. "Do you remember," he said, "when I came I could not take my empty cereal bowl to the kitchen without getting milk on the ceiling? Now I can serve the slipperiest dessert you can make."

3. *Let all other introductory steps wait upon the development of the learner's attitude toward a learning situation.* Regardless of what research may ultimately reveal about the function of attitude in total performance, we are convinced that the first task in any attempt at new learning is in the area of attitude. A child who does something under duress, to please somebody, for reward, or to avoid punishment, learns with little energy at his disposal. Rayswift children have taught us this again and again by the rapid changes they wrought in their doings—social, academic, and physical—as they were helped to a feeling favorable to growth.

Translated into a classroom teaching situation this means that an introduction to a subject field or project is most advantageous when it is spent in concern for attitudes toward the task and the stabilization of purpose to engage in it. We distinguish between half-hearted and whole-hearted participation. When desire to do or have has become whole-hearted, the child has his whole self to focus upon it.

4. *Trust cooperation as the major technique of growth and development.* We have learned for certain that children accomplish more through cooperation than through competition. Whether it be building a diving stand for the lake, or prettying up the horse for the horse show, what is done together yields more in human values than children pitted against each other. We are

satisfied that competition with one's fellow, rather than cooperation with him, is a tool of defensiveness.

Teachers who experiment with cooperative technique begin by being surprised at the way in which the purposes and projects engaged in by children tend to fall into the form in which the adults would have directed them.

Certain of our learnings are less tangible than those referred to above but are nonetheless potent. These matters are difficult to verbalize, and more difficult to defend, since they do not lend themselves to conventional scientific procedures and laboratory methods. These we choose to state as our present convictions. If they provoke discussion, they will the more readily come to clarification.

Certain environmental "climates" are more favorable for growth than others. For example, the general climate (not necessarily related to specific words or avowed pronouncements) in which the child can be sure of his importance to someone is most favorable to his skills in social behavior. Rayswift children are as curious about strangers as any other children. They crowd around to see who has arrived, or who is being served tea or ice cream. They are introduced and the guests described as "so-and-so's mother," or "Dr. Rasey's friends from the university." After two or three minutes the children are invited to go on. They always go without fuss. Their wishes were respected in being told who the guests were. They are so sure of their places with us, and their importance to us, that they do not have to prove them to themselves. Their wishes were respected so they respect ours in requesting them to go.

The climate in which it is recognized that breakable things will break, and that there are blame-free, right ways to take care of such things, lets Rayswift children grow skillful in acknowledging responsibility for an accident, or even a disobedience. It often goes like this. "I was playing ball and I broke the garage window." Sometimes they report at the same time, "I told Al and he is going to fix it before dark." If the latter comment is not forthcoming, we may say, "I'm glad you reported it. What have you done about it?" If he hasn't known what to do, he is instructed. Sometimes he asks, "Should I pay for it?" Countered by, "What do you think?" If his reply is evasive, time is taken to clarify the issue. If payment for the entire cost of the damage would exhaust his resources, a suggestion is made as to how a reasonable contribution could be made. This method is sometimes used if the individual says he was careless, or if he is a frequent repeater. A child has a better social technique if he knows what to do to make good an accident than if he is told what he must do as punishment.

The climate is kept on the constructive and positive side as far as may be without becoming sentimental. A child gradually becomes habituated to seeing and appraising a problem situation or circumstance in terms of what there is in it with which to alter it. One of the children put it succinctly when a problem arose with several children wanting pop when only a half-bottle remained. "Can't you see that the bottle is half-empty?" one of us asked. "Yes, I can see that," the child responded, "but it is also half-full and the half-full part is what we want."

The climate referred to here is favorable to the less able as well as the more able. Handicaps of others—age, sickness, inability of any kind—are discussed in terms of the responsibility of the more for the less able. "Someone should ride beside Henry. He does not hear well." People occupied with discovering how they can be useful have less energy available to tease, or torment, which is perhaps the commonest of heedless responses to the less able. It seems to us a mistake to say children are cruel. We think they are merely inexperienced. We try to let no serious crippledness or ugliness come upon them unaware. When a child with a facial blemish was coming, the other children were told that such a child was coming. "She might not like it if we talked about it." The answer was instantaneous: "Let's don't then." And they didn't. One day when a heedless adult said, "What's the matter with the little girl's face?" One of the youngest answered, "It's a birthmark, but we don't talk about it."

We have been interested to see how this attitude grows into a concern for other living things—cats and flowers and the like.

"Perky," said Nancy, "is the cat's name. We call her Perky and she doesn't know she is a cat. She thinks she is a people."

The climate is one in which relevances are kept orderly. They inquire if it will hurt when disinfectant goes into a cut, or when they go to the dentist. They are told yes it will, perhaps, but that isn't the point. We believe that the children "take in" from the atmosphere a certain logic about more things than cuts and the dentist. A newcomer boy demurred about his share of the dish washing, because it was "girl's work." Another child answered, "You liked to dirty them, didn't you—or was that 'girl's work' too?"

This climate is heavily laden with the "3 L's." They live and love and learn. They want a share in most things. They learn to put themselves into things. They learn to laugh at their own mistakes rather than those of others. This helps them to lay down their "mis-take" more gracefully and to take again. Those whose experiences have not made them good lovers are helped to that skill. They have birds and beasts and bushes and flowers, as well as the works of their hands and their fellows and their adults. Those who learn to love have good life insurance.

From our experience we have incorporated into our own doing and can recommend to others the following climatic conditions:

1. It is helpful to treat children with the kind of concern and seriousness with which we like to be treated.

2. It is helpful for a child to live in an atmosphere in which he can make his own mistakes gracefully and be courageous enough to profit by them. He, like ourselves, tends to alter or adorn the truth when he feels the inequality of himself and the truth as it is.

3. The child will tend to emphasize in his values that which he finds others emphasizing. When one child complained about the taste of the medicine given him another said, "If you like it or don't isn't important. It's whether it does what it's supposed to."

4. Just keeping alive in our pell-mell world is an achievement. When that has been routinized the real task comes, that of living abundantly. The skill to do this lies more largely in one's *interpretation* of his environment than in the actual richness

of it. One learns to love by being associated with good lovers. It may be ungrammatical to love rabbits and rugs, flowers and fruit, people and people, but it is excellent life philosophy.

Still other learnings which we value lie in even less well defined areas than those here discussed. These learnings came and remained as questions raised rather than as questions answered. They are centered around concepts often considered axiomatic. These questions raise obstacles in paths of thought long considered straight and smooth. They are not—or at least, not yet—in a state of crystallization which permits formulation of hypotheses for testing. They are intentions, perhaps even hunches. These questions are difficult to state because they derive from experience which is either so well digested as to have dropped below (or risen above) rule-of-thumb statement, or so poorly digested as to keep them still formless. If our statements of these issues are to prove serviceable to anyone besides ourselves they will be used, as we now use them, to forge tools for further investigation, or to act as wedges in opening up fresh areas.

Intensive study in any area of human behavior is likely to bring up evidence of conflict between the basic concepts with which we look and the evidence we see as we look. In the course of this study, and particularly in reviewing the records, we have had occasion to question accepted premises again and again.

We count these questions so raised of great value to us, and to any who care to consider them. They point to unexplored territory. They suggest basic errors in concepts which, should the questioning be valid, would call for some major rethinking. We have few answers to these questions. Where we think we have found them, we have already presented them in the text. There remains at this point only the task of rehearsing these questions. Some of them have value chiefly in reminding us of the vast unexplored areas of human capacity whose nearer boundaries are scarcely defined and whose remoter ones are unguessed.

Certain of these questions make our fingers itch for funds and facilities for running down the answers. We wish we were free to find out the nature of this dynamic growth on the levels not so far explored. We wish we were free to pursue for another five years those uniquenesses of the so-called superior child.

We feel that many superior children fail to grow into superior adults because teachers know too little about the culture of such personalities and the children go flat and unproductive. We wish we could devote ourselves to next steps in pursuing the things we guess, to determine whether they can be verified as facts or must be abandoned as follies. These and a hundred others like them clamor for study. These are questions for which we know how to find answers. Only labor lies between them and their solutions.

But there are other problems so complex and so farreaching that no one or two persons are likely to make much headway with them. We are obligated nonetheless to state them. For example, there is something wrong with the contrast between the places usually given to feeling and to reason. Scientists have held for some time that functioning of the central nervous system in the cerebral areas was of a higher order than that of the "old brain" with its concomitant or correlated function with smooth muscle, endocrine systems, and the rest. Yet the acceptance of a behavior by an individual and the release of his energy to its performance is dependent in last analysis on a *right feeling*—not a right reason! Have we misfigured the respective roles of these two segments of the nervous system? Is it possible that these ancient feelings, automatized and relatively independent of cerebration, represent our greatest wisdom? Have we possibly mistaken reason, essentially the blue-print maker, for the architect? Need we reappraise these functions of the nervous systems? We see also that feeling outruns reason in its management of total energy. Under stress of feeling the organism sometimes does what apparently "could not be done." What is in fact the potential of this organism, viewed in the light of its occasional achievement? We do not get far with this speculation until we must question the comparative worth of the product of reason with the product of intuition, when the latter is defined in terms of the organism's own unconscious knowings.

Sherrington illustrates a specific aspect of the question we are posing here when he comments on "altruism as passion . . . nature's noblest product; the greatest contribution made by man to Life. . . . At first glance such altruism may strike the biologist as contrary to the broad trend . . . of life. That makes the more notable the fact that evolution nevertheless has brought it about. . . . It is well to note it is not essentially rational. It is often more germane to emotion than to intellect. It belongs, if you will to sentiment, and it can elevate sentiment so that intellect at best ranks but as a tool for sentiment. It creates a reasoned emotion. It may have the conquest of the world before it, in which case reason will play its part, as a tool."[1]

What if such "intuitional knowings" should prove to be residual types of learning, laid down in nerve fiber, colloid, and humor from remoter knowings? Along with Sherrington, Aurobindo suggests that mind and reason are not our highest distinction from the beasts. Suppose the latter is right in his statement that "mind is only a preparatory form of our consciousness, an instrument of analysis and synthesis, but not of essential knowledge. . . . Mind is a passage not a culmination."[2]

These and like questions plague us as time after time we find discrepancies between what occurs in human behavior and the conceptual hierarchies with which we are accustomed to interpret our observations. At this point we are inclined to say, with Kelley, that although we are confused, "we think we are confused about more important things, and on higher levels."[3]

[1] Sir Charles Sherrington, *Man on His Nature* (New York: The Macmillan Company, 1941).
[3] Earl C. Kelley, *The Workshop of Learning* (New York: Harper & Brothers, 1951).

INDEX

163